COPYWRITING
BY DESIGN

COPYWRITING BY DESIGN

Bringing Ideas To Life With Words And Images

David Herzbrun

NTC Business Books
a division of *NTC Publishing Group* • Lincolnwood, Illinois USA

Library of Congress Cataloging-in-Publication Data

Herzbrun, David.
   Copywriting by design : bringing ideas to life with words and
images / David Herzbrun.
     p.   cm.
   ISBN 0-8442-3671-3 (paper)
   1. Advertising copy. 2. Advertising layout and typography.
3. Commerical art. I. Title.
HF5825.H48 1996
659.13′2—dc20   96-28167
                                                  CIP

Published by NTC Business Books, a division of NTC Publishing Group
4255 West Touhy Avenue
Lincolnwood (Chicago), Illinois 60646-1975, U.S.A.
67890 VL 987654321

Contents

PART THREE: Putting Words into Action

PART FOUR: Creating Reality from Thin Air

PART FIVE: The Great Outdoors

PART SIX: The Bottom Line for You

Foreword

This book was written to help students of copywriting and art direction. Art and design students who are future advertising art directors may choose to skip the parts that teach the somewhat primitive basics of drawing and lettering. Designers know that already. But the odds are that few of them know how to use their skills to *communicate*.

In advertising, communication is becoming more visual all the time. That doesn't mean it's nonverbal, but it does mean that the words and the pictures must work together. That unity is the theme of this book. Its title, *Copywriting by Design*, is a phrase that puts the two parts of an ad—the visual and the verbal—in one thought.

Part One

What's the Big Idea?

See What I Mean

In this chapter you will

- learn why images have become so important.
- discover how images communicate.
- see some perfect visual/verbal marriages.

Turn on your TV and turn off the sound. Now watch some commercials. You might wish you could hear the music for some of them, but the odds are you won't miss the words.

For the past three decades, since TV entered our lives, we've been learning more every year about how to communicate visually.

Until the late 1960s the standard commercial length was sixty seconds. Most of those commercials were pretty wordy affairs; they were often no more than radio commercials with pictures. Later, as air time became more expensive, thirty seconds became the standard commercial length, and that's not much time to get a logical, well-reasoned sales message across. More recently, advertisers have cut costs even further by using fifteen-second commercials.

By necessity, then, we learned how to use pictures to communicate a message. In turn, viewers learned how to react to them. In fact, they've learned so well that they've almost forgotten how to react to basic, verbal selling messages that communicate nothing without the words.

What's an ad-maker to do? Communicate.

To begin, you must learn to stop thinking of yourself as a writer or an art director. Start thinking of yourself as a *communicator*. Your job is to get a message across, by whatever means it takes—words, symbols, pictures, or a combination of these, plus music or dance or animated raisins. Whatever works.

"But I'm a *writer*," I can hear some of you thinking. "I don't know how to draw or make a layout. My education is in words, not pictures." And others of you are thinking, "Hey, I'm a *designer*. I don't know a thing about writing headlines."

Wrong.

Whatever your discipline, you're part of the audience, too. You've been *receiving* visual and verbal messages since you were born, and you can learn to *send* visual and verbal messages as naturally and easily as you receive them.

In learning this skill, you'll be broadening your vocabulary—your communication vocabulary. Our normal verbal vocabulary—the words we actually use, not the much larger vocabulary of words we can read and understand—totals about 6,000, give or take a few hundred. But our visual vocabulary is vastly larger and is more universal.

In experimenting with quick-cut TV spots, it has been shown that the average viewer can identify and remember pictures that flash by at the rate of *three per second*. When you add visuals to your vocabulary and learn to marry words with your images, your ability to communicate grows enormously.

Just as the right picture can reinforce your ads, it can even replace words, so that the words you do use become more important. Is one picture really worth 1,000 words? I'll believe it when someone can convey that thought in a picture.

What I do believe is that one picture, married to a few of the right words, is better than a thousand words or a hundred pictures.

Of course, pictures do communicate. But how? Here's a simple example:

> Visualize the classic cartoon situation where a tattered traveler, crawling across a desert, sees a mirage on the horizon.
> In this case, the mirage is a frosty bottle of Pepsi.

What should the headline say? What should the body copy say? Do you need either?

In this example the picture tells the whole story. It gets your attention. It sets up the problem, shows the solution, and attempts to sell the product by communicating a benefit.

Unfortunately, this isn't a good example of effective advertising. The situation is overused and the benefit it promises is so ordinary that it's generic. However, it is an excellent example of how much can be communicated without writing a word.

Imagine how powerfully that picture would work if it had grown out of a fresh and relevant selling proposition. If that were the case, then it should be possible to write a headline that would breathe new life into the picture.

To explain what I mean by that, I'm going to tell you about a few classic ad campaigns from the ad agency Doyle Dane Bernbach, where I worked during the "Creative Revolution" of the 1960s. We taught the public to think small for Volkswagen, tore a strip off a photo of the Atlantic Ocean to show that El Al Airlines was 10 percent faster to Europe, and made Avis try harder.

One ad that I created for Volkswagen provides as good an example as I know of how words and pictures work best when they are fully integrated.

Some shapes are hard to improve on.

Ask any hen.
You just can't design a more functional shape for an egg.
And we figure the same is true of the Volkswagen Sedan.
Don't think we haven't tried.
(As a matter of fact, the Volkswagen's been changed nearly 3,000 times.)

But we can't improve our basic design. Like the egg, it's the right kind of package for what goes inside.
So that's where most of our energy goes.
To get more power without using more gas. To put synchromesh on first gear. To improve the heater. That kind of thing.

As a result, our package carries four adults, and their luggage, at about 32 miles to a gallon of regular gas and 40,000 miles to a set of tires.
We've made a few external changes, of course. Such as push-button doorknobs.
Which is one up on the egg.

As you see, the picture doesn't mean a thing without the headline, except to point out that the car is somewhat egg-shaped. The headline is equally meaningless without that picture. But together, they powerfully communicate a message that Volkswagen management wanted to get across to a public that was getting a little bored with the car's unchanging and homely looks.

That Volkswagen ad first appeared in 1963. Here's another ad that first appeared in 1993 that works in much the same way.

Both of these ads are the result of visual/verbal *thinking* and not of compartmental thinking, where the art director waits for the copywriter to come up with a headline and then reaches for a sketch pad.

Before getting started on creating ads and campaigns that use the visual/verbal link, there are a few basics you have to know first. We'll begin to lay this groundwork in the next chapter.

In this chapter you've learned how pictures communicate and how they communicate better when married to the right words. Perhaps more important, you've learned that your job is not writing or designing but communicating.

CHAPTER 2

Why Advertising?

In this chapter you will

- discover that advertising can do many things.
- learn how strategy affects creative.
- meet the target market.
- understand a positioning statement.

Most people will tell you that the purpose of advertising is sales. This is certainly true in retail advertising, where the cash register tells you at the end of the day how well the ad worked. Sales are also the sole measure of effectiveness in direct response advertising, such as mail-order catalogs and mailings and print ads that carry coupons that ask you to mail or phone in an order. There the ad must do the whole selling job, without the help of a salesperson or a product you can examine, touch, and try on. But generating the immediate sale of a product or a service is only one of the many reasons to advertise.

The Many Purposes of Advertising

Advertising does many things. Consider automobile advertising. It is largely intended to create a favorable opinion of the brand, not to sell a particular model. Most of the potential customers aren't in the market for a car when they see the magazine ad or the TV commercial, but when they are at last ready to buy, if the campaign worked well, the brand will be one of several on their consideration list. The real selling will be done at the car dealership. The objective of that advertising was simply to get the prospects into the showroom.

Another example of the multifunctionality of advertising is corporate advertising, often called image advertising. Corporate advertising is most often intended to increase awareness and create a favorable image of the company in the financial community. However, it may have other, more obscure jobs to do as well.

One of my clients was a major oil company who was afraid that environmental groups might force the government to enact legislation that would overly restrict oil exploration and development. To address this concern, we created a campaign of TV commercials aimed at a tiny audience—the leaders of the White House and members of key committees in Congress, at the Sierra Club, and at other environmental groups.

The audience was so small that we knew all of their names; we could have written a letter to each of them. We chose, however, to use television instead, because a letter from an oil company was more likely to anger these people than to soothe them. We wanted our audience to feel that a larger public was being addressed.

The commercials were documentaries that showed the care the company was taking to protect the environment all around the world. The purpose of the campaign was not to sell or even to make something happen. It's real purpose was to *prevent* something from happening.

So before you start thinking of making an ad, you must first think of who your target audience is going to be and how you want to affect their behavior or attitudes. This is called an advertising strategy.

The Advertising Strategy Is Your Guide

An advertising strategy provides all of the essential information that the advertiser and the ad agency account manager, research manager, and media director have agreed that you need to know.

The Target Market

Most advertising strategies begin with a description of the consumers, the target market for the product. The description will contain both demographic and psychographic elements.

Demographics Demographics are statistics that tell you the age, income, race, and sex of the target, whether or not there are children in the household, where they live, if there is a regional bias in their distribution, whether they are urban, suburban, or rural, and whatever other facts you need to know.

Psychographics Psychographics tell you about the target's self-image, lifestyle, mood while using the product or a competitive one, how the product fulfills a need (other than the obvious, practical need), and other relevant data.

The Positioning Statement

The advertising strategy's centerpiece is a positioning statement. The positioning statement is a brief paragraph, preferably no more than a single sentence, that states why the advertiser wants people to think about the product or service to be advertised.

The standard, preferred form is structured as follows: "For (target audience), (product name) is (principal claim) because (main support for claim)." Using this format, a completed positioning statement for a mythical product might read:

> "For men and women between 16 and 26, Rock-Buster Jeans are the best hiking and climbing wear, because they have reinforced seats and knees."

The following is the positioning statement for an imaginary product, Grand Tour Soups, with which you'll be dealing throughout this book:

"For people who like classic foreign soups, Grand Tour makes authentic soups not available in canned form in their countries of origin."

Notice that this positioning statement contains no "because" support. This isn't uncommon in food and beverage products, where the only payoff is taste, not logic.

Goal of the Advertising

The goal of the advertising should be identified in the advertising strategy. What is the advertising trying to accomplish? For example, the purpose of advertising Grand Tour Soups will be to stimulate trial. If the products deliver what you promise, you've got a winner. If they don't, nothing will save them. (Advertising creative pioneer Bill Bernbach once said, "Great advertising is the quickest way to kill a bad product.")

Media Strategy

The advertising strategy will also include media strategy that identifies the media for which you'll be creating advertising. The media strategy tells you if you will be working with newspapers, magazines, radio, TV, outdoor billboards, or a combination of these. It will also tell you if the publications will be mass or targeted and what kind of environment will be sought out in radio and television.

Other Considerations

Where mood and occasion are meaningful parts of the communication, the advertising strategy will spell them out.

Usage How is the product to be used by the target market? For example, will Grand Tour Soups be consumed alone, with the family, or with company? Will they be eaten only before the meal, or will they serve as the main course of a light meal? Will the mood be festive or homey?

Tone A good advertising strategy will specify a tone for the advertising. It may be "sophisticated, wise, and worldly," "newsy and urgent," "warm and friendly," "elegant and upscale," cheerful and good-humored," etc.

The Integrated Marketing Communications Plan

A complete strategy will also include an integrated marketing communications plan. The integrated marketing communications plan outlines strategies designed to link together sales promotion, packaging, trade advertising, publicity and public relations activities, and any other communications elements by a common theme.

Finally, the advertising strategy will often be accompanied by a few appendices, such as consumer research data, competitive advertising proofs and storyboards, a brand-by-brand market review, pricing strategy, estimated frequency of product usage, and other data.

Read the Plan!

Don't skip any part of the advertising strategy plan. A single insight from a consumer, perhaps half-buried in a research study, may become the illuminating truth that is the heart and soul of your ad campaign.

If all this sound confining and constricting to your creativity, I assure you that quite the contrary is true. It's easier to be creative when you know what to be creative about. To fully understand how much an advertising strategy effects the creative outcome, complete the following assignment.

Assignment

Your product is a sturdy touring bicycle that is intended for transportation and exercise, as opposed to trail bikes, racing bikes, and mountain bikes.

You are to create two ads:

#1. • Target audience: men and women aged 19–39.
    • Medium: *Rolling Stone*, color page.

#2. • Target audience: men and women aged 55–65.
    • Medium: *Modern Maturity*, color page.

It should be immediately obvious that you can't simply take a single advertising idea and shoot it with models of different ages. The two market groups will most likely buy the bike for different reasons, and you need to address those reasons in your ads. Your first job is to imagine what these reasons for buying might be. Next, think of how to communicate the message to each audience.

Because you haven't read this book yet, create these ads by writing a headline and by describing what you'd like to do visually. Don't make a layout, don't draw, and don't write any copy except the headline and, if necessary, a subhead, which is usually either a support or a clarification of the headline.

For example, the following classic headline/subhead combination launched Clairol's success and was the heart of their campaign for many years:

HEADLINE: **Does she or doesn't she?**
SUBHEAD: Color so natural, only her hairdresser knows for
           sure.

In this chapter you've learned that advertising can do many things and that the job of any ad or campaign is spelled out in a strategy that defines the target audience and the message.

New Key Terms

* demographics

* direct response

* integrated marketing communications plan

* positioning statement

* psychographics

* target market

 **CHAPTER 3**

Where Do Ideas Come From?

In this chapter you will

- discover the value of consumer research.
- learn the difference between an idea and an ad.
- learn how to grow an idea.
- start to think visually.

Good advertising ideas don't come from anywhere; they've been there all along. Most them are built right into the product or service in the form of quality, price, or competitive advantage. Others are in the target market—your customer's needs, hopes, dreams, and fears.

The best advertising ideas are not immediately obvious. How do you find them?

Research the Product or Service

You'll have to start with some homework. Read the strategy and learn all that you can about the product or service. Ask for a tour of the factory or workplace. Talk (and listen closely) to the person in charge. Ask whether the manufacturing process or the customer relations includes any procedure, design, or safety advantage that competing products don't have.

At the Volkswagen factory in Germany, I asked why the wheels on the VW Beetle were noticeably bigger than those on other small cars. I thought the reason might be for a smoother ride, which would make for a fairly boring claim. To my surprise, I was told that big wheels result in better fuel mileage. And that made a fine ad.

Equally important as the search for unique facts, look for strong selling points that are not unique to the product but that aren't being advertised by competitors.

For example, all gasolines contain a detergent, but nobody ever told the public about it until Mobil Oil's "drive your engine clean" campaign. Mobil has been "the detergent gasoline" for many years now, and no other product can take the claim away from them.

Get to Know the Target

After you've learned all about the product or service, learn everything you can about the target market. Get inside the head of your target consumer.

A good way to start is by reading the qualitative research, which is a report or reports on focus groups. Focus groups are typically composed of ten people who have been carefully screened by recruiters to match the characteristics of the target market. These individuals are led in discussion for an hour or two by a trained moderator who inconspicuously follows a discussion guide. The moderator takes notes and makes an audio tape of the discussion.

When the focus groups are completed, the moderator will write a report, including findings, conclusions, and recommendations. When reading this report, don't just read the findings, conclusions, and recommendations. Read the "verbatims," which are direct quotes from target audience members. If you have the time, listen to some of the tapes. When you feel you have a thorough understanding of your target, pair this knowledge with the product knowledge and then watch the ideas flow.

An Idea Is Not an Ad

Of course an idea isn't an ad, but it is raw stuff from which ads are made. There are many ways of going about the making of an ad—logical appeal, emotional appeal, long copy, short copy, inclusion of a response coupon, and so on—but the idea, not the execution, is what will motivate consumers.

One historical ad comes to mind. In 1916, the great copywriter, Claude Hopkins, had to come up with an idea for Sunkist. Oranges were used at that time primarily as a fruit to eat. Through consumer research, Hopkins found that people loved oranges but didn't eat very many because they were messy and drippy. He squeezed a few and found they made a great drink. He reasoned that they would be used more often if the drink were advertised.

No matter what advertising execution you can think of, there's nothing you can do to hurt an idea as strong as that.

What he did do was create a Hopkins-style ad consisting of long copy and a big insert offering an orange juice "extractor" for a dime. I'm certain this ad would have worked just as well with a big appetizing picture of a glass of juice and his headline: "Drink an orange." It would have worked on radio and TV if they had been around then, and it would have worked on outdoor billboards and on in-store displays.

Hopkins' idea changed an industry. This example is a perfect illustration of the power of an idea. Think how often the whole world has been changed by an idea.

How to Grow an Idea

In advertising, very few ideas come as personal revelations, but there are reasonable, logical ways to develop them. The method I will cover here is based on visual conceptualization.

Whether you're a writer or a designer, you're used to thinking in words. Now you're going to learn to think *without words* and without drawing pictures.

Let's start with an advertising assignment we touched on earlier and that you're going to revisit in all media through the course of this book—the introduction of a new line of canned soups called Grand Tour Soups. Let's begin with the strategy.

- **The target market** is men and women aged 29 to 49 with household incomes over $50,000.

- **The media** will be primarily home-oriented magazines, plus seasonal support on TV and radio. The launch campaign will include point of sale and money-off coupons in FSI's (Free Standing Inserts) in newspaper coupon carriers. After the launch, outdoor advertising will be phased in.

- **The message** your client wants to send is identified in the following positioning statement:

     Grand Tour Soups are the world's only canned soups made from authentic and delicious international recipes.

- **The support** is that you can't buy canned soups like these, even in the countries where they originated.

The line includes Parisian Onion, Hong Kong Hot & Sour, Seville Gazpacho, Acapulco Black Bean, Athenian Egg-Lemon, Black Forest Bean & Ham, and Aberdeen Lamb and Barley. Research shows that most consumers will try the Parisian Onion Soup first, so that's what you'll feature in your first ad.

Think Visually

Now, let's start to think visually. What do we want to *show* in the ad? We'll probably want to show a bowl of steaming soup, if only for appetite appeal, but you know that's not a very distinctive picture. This image just communicates "soup" and not your *main point of difference*, which is "international." We'll want to show something to communicate "international" or, even better, "French" or, more specifically, "Parisian." What can you think of?

It's time for you to start working on your visual vocabulary. What pictures say "Parisian" to you? The Eiffel Tower? Notre Dame Cathedral? The Arc de Triomphe? Lovers sitting at a sidewalk cafe or walking under the chestnut blossoms by the river Seine? Do any of them have anything to do with soup? If they don't, keep thinking.

Have you considered a French person tasting soup with a pleased expression? This may sound dumb, but it's not such a bad idea. People are usually more interested in other people than in products. But whose face should it be?

A man or a woman? A little kid? A gendarme? A grandma? How about a French movie star or a famous French athlete?

Maybe, instead of just a face, it's a whole scene with many happy faces. You could show a family eating soup at a dining table in a room with a big window that frames a view of the Eiffel tower in the distance. Or is that too complicated?

Can you think of a visual that communicates more than just "Parisian" and "soup"? Can you think of something that communicates "delicious" and "authentic" as well? How about a French cook in his chef's hat, tasting the soup with a surprised and delighted look?

Every one of those visual ideas communicates something different. In my opinion, the French chef works harder than the others. It communicates "authentically French" and "good tasting" and "authoritative." And there's another reason I like it—it can be "pooled out" to make a campaign.

Does Your Idea Pool Out?

An idea is said to "pool out" if it leads easily from one execution to another in all media. The chef idea does it. The next ad can show a Chinese chef tasting Hong Kong Hot & Sour Soup, followed by an ad with a Spanish chef tasting Seville Gazpacho, and on and on to create as many ads as Grand Tour has soups.

Think about it. This campaign could work very well on TV, too. Can you visualize a TV commercial? Take a moment to try. You're going to have to create one later, when we work together on TV.

The foreign chef campaign could also make some interesting, distinctive radio. Give a few minutes of thought to what the radio might sound like. You're going to create that, too, later on. When you think about radio now, don't forget the music and the sound effects. They're radio's equivalent of pictures. And now think about some great looking outdoor posters. Not hard to do, right?

A campaign that pools out in many different media and in many executions is also said to have "legs." This one is a regular centipede. It could even work well in sales promotion, such as a Grand Tour sweepstakes with travel prizes.

Of course, you may come up with an idea you like better than mine. For example, you might want to do an ad featuring a really complicated and time-consuming recipe, with the headline: "Or try Grand Tour Parisian Onion Soup." Or you might want to show a couple at a contemporary breakfast area table and chairs, in a room that looks like a Parisian cafe. Your headline might be: "It happens to our kitchen every time we taste Grand Tour Parisian Onion Soup." Maybe you have a different idea altogether. But since I don't know what it is, I'll have to show you how to do mine.

Bringing the Idea Down to Earth

We have already decided to have two main pictures: one will be a French chef, and the other will be a steaming bowl of soup. We've also decided that the chef will make for more interesting, distinctive, and communicative advertising than the bowl of soup. The chef, then, will be the dominant visual. Remember, though, that the bowl of soup can't be a little throwaway, the size of a postage stamp. Its job is to look appetizing, and it has to be big enough to do the job.

So you already know that the layout has to make room for a big picture and a medium-sized picture. But that's not all. Grand Tour Soups are a new line, and customers have to know what to look for on the grocery shelf. That means that another visual—a can of soup that's big enough to identify—is needed.

And you must still consider more visual elements. Where is the headline going to go? How much space will it occupy? Maybe you'll need a subhead, and then there's copy. How many words will you need to write? Copy is more than just words. It's a visual element, too, because it occupies space.

When you've thought about all of this, you can make a list of the visuals you'll need. Here's my list:

- A big picture of a chef
- A smaller picture of a bowl of soup
- A picture of a can, big enough to read
- A headline
- A subhead
- Four or five lines of copy in type about the size of this book type.

Stop right now and consider what we've done. We've conceived visually! We've done it without making a layout or drawing anything, and we haven't even had to write a headline.

In this chapter you've learned the value of consumer research and how it can lead you to ideas that can grow into ads. Most important, you've learned how to think visually.

New Key Terms

✳ legs

✳ pool out

✳ qualitative research

✳ verbatims

Part Two

Bringing the Visuals to Life

CHAPTER 4

If You're Not a Designer, Don't Act Like One

In this chapter you will

- reshape a classic layout.
- learn how to indicate type.
- see how a layout grows from an idea.
- find an assortment of sample layouts.

Now it's time for you to make your layout. Copywriters, don't panic. Before you even think about it, I want you to absorb one simple, but very big, idea. Memorize it as a guiding principle. It's the title of this chapter: *If you're not a designer, don't act like one.* If you're a writer, don't ever try to make an original layout. Don't even think about it. This is an absolute rule.

Start With a Classic layout

This layout is a familiar classic.

The boxed area with an X through it indicates where a picture will appear. The headlines, subheads, and logos are indicated by loopy strokes like these:

Sometimes they're shown in angular, V-shaped strokes, like these:

When you start drawing layouts, you may find that the angular strokes have one advantage over the loops. It's easy to keep them in a straight line by placing a rule on the page and stopping each downstroke of your pencil with the edge of the ruler.

Copy is indicated by lines like these:

This classic layout features a big picture that takes up about two thirds to three quarters of a page. The headline is centered under the picture, with equal space above and below it.

David Ogilvy used this layout with great success for many accounts, including Hathaway shirts, British Travel Association, Schweppes Tonic, and the Commonwealth of Puerto Rico. All these campaigns ran at the same time and all were outstandingly successful.

Many advertising professionals criticized these look-alikes as being uncreative. But when Doyle Dane Bernbach's great art director, Helmut Krone, used the same layout for the Volkswagen Beetle campaign, it was hailed as a creative breakthrough.

Here's one of David Ogilvy's ads:

The newest part of Salisbury Cathedral is its spire. It is over 600 years old.

How to hear the music of an old cathedral town

AFTER TRAVELLING all day, most people long for five simple things. A friendly welcome. A hot bath. A good dinner. A comfortable night's lodging. And *peace*.

Britain's great cathedral towns have provided these creature comforts for centuries. They still do.

Imagine arriving in Salisbury on the evening our photograph was taken. The first thing you notice is the peace. It isn't a dumb silence but a gentle harmony of sounds. The whirr of a lawn mower. The slippered footsteps of devout men. The creak of praying oaks.

You find your inn and the music changes. There's a promise of refreshment in the jolly clunk of beer pumps. A promise of good fellowship in the sunburned country laughter. And a promise of good cheer in the kitchen chatter of dishes. The menu looks so tempting that you hurry down to dinner and postpone your bath. Ah well.

Salisbury is only one of thirty great cathedral towns that offer the same sort of welcome. Some travelers plan their tours so that they stay at a cathedral town every night. It makes delightful sense. Ask your travel-agent.

For free color booklet, "Old Towns of Britain," see your travel agent or write Box 134, British Travel Association.
In New York—680 Fifth Avenue. In Los Angeles—606 South Hill St.; In Chicago—39 South La Salle St.; In Canada—90 Adelaide Street West, Toronto.

Here's one of Helmut Krone's early Volkswagen ads:

Any similarity between the cathedral town ad and the Volkswagen ad is only superficial.

Remember, a layout is no more than a packing crate. What really counts is what you put in it. If you're a copywriter looking for your first job, more than half of your portfolio could use this classic layout.

If your concepts and your writing are smart, no creative director will say a negative word about the layouts. Design students need to design something fresh, but don't get carried away with graphic whiz-bangs. You and the copywriters should learn one great principle. *Let the layout grow from the idea.*

Let the Layout Grow

You'll see how layouts grow from ideas as we put one together for Grand Tour Parisian Onion Soup.

The tools and supplies you'll need are:

- A pad of tracing paper (14″ × 17″)

- Some soft, black pencils

- Some soft-tipped pens (fine, medium, and heavy)

- A plastic, drafting 90-degree triangle

- A kneaded eraser

- Some typing paper

Instead of creating a full-sized layout, we'll start with a smaller, "thumbnail," layout. We will work in thumbnails because most of us, even professional art directors, find they're a lot easier to draw— and to throw away—than full pages.

Make your thumbnail in whatever size you feel comfortable working, from postage stamp (too small for me) to half actual size (too large for me). Take your pencil and a sheet of tracing paper and noodle around a while. Decide what size of thumbnail feels good to you.

To get started on Grand Tour Soups, let's see if our classic layout is of any use, knowing already that we'll have to modify it to make room for the bowl of soup and the can.

Here's a first thumbnail:

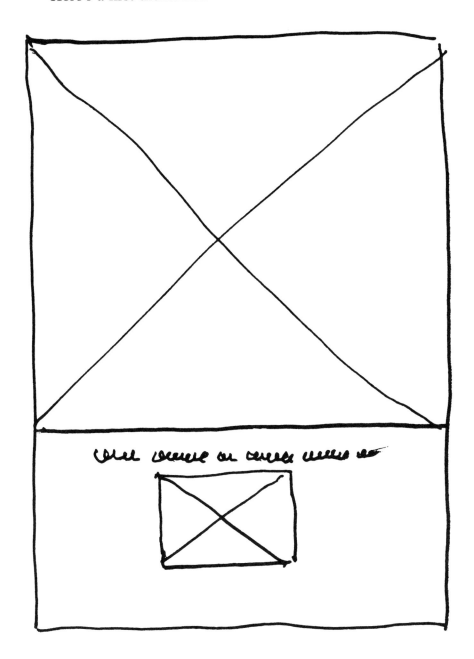

Somehow it doesn't look right, does it? What's wrong? Maybe it's the fact that we can't tell right away whether the headline relates to the big picture or the small one. Another problem is deciding where to put the short block of copy and the can of soup. Suppose we decided to make the headline a quote from the French chef? If we did that, it would look natural at the top of the page, just over his head.

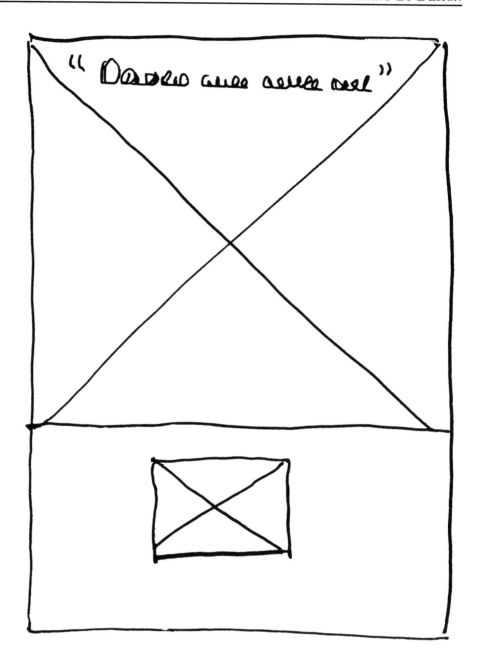

That's a lot better. But now we need something to connect these two pictures and to lead the eye from the headline and main picture to the small picture and copy. Let's put in a subhead.

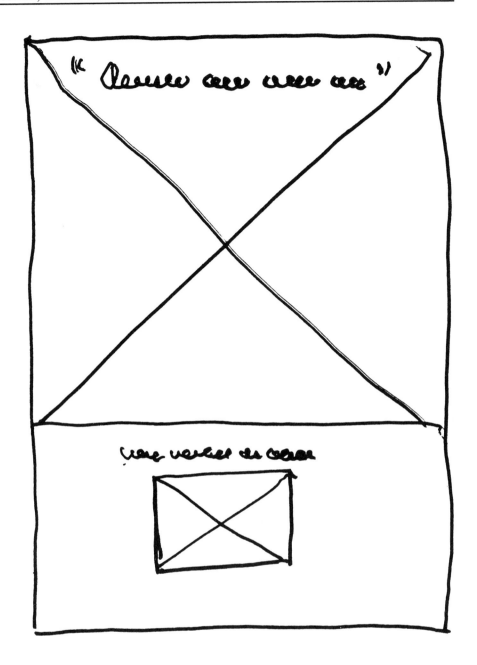

Finally, let's see what it looks like with the soup can in the usual place to show packages, on the lower right, with the copy in four lines on the left.

To my eye it looks out of balance. Let's try the bowl of soup on the left of the page to balance the can on the right. That way, we can stretch out the copy between the two smaller pictures and lead the reader's eye in a logical way.

Now it looks like an ad, doesn't it? Or at least it looks like a blueprint for an ad. There are quite a few more possibilities that would work to include a major and a minor picture, a product shot, a headline, and some short copy. Look through a few magazines and see if you can find one or two to swipe. "Swipe" is a legitimate word in advertising. Every art director and every illustrator keeps a "swipe file" and would have a fit if it was stolen.

To help you start a swipe file of your own, the following pages will show you a variety of standard layouts that answer most needs. You'll get some ideas about how to handle long copy ad and ads with almost no copy. There are layouts to use when several small pictures are needed, and there are layouts for two-page spreads, full-pages, half-pages, quarter-pages, and columns. Feel free to steal what you need.

The Use of Type

Did you notice the different ways that type is used in these layouts? Some used *justified* type, sometimes called "flush right and left," which sets copy in lines of exactly the same length until a paragraph ends, like this:

Some are set flush left and uneven right, usually called "*rag* (for ragged) *right*," like this:

_____

_____

_____

_____

_____

_____

_____

_____

Setting type rag right avoids breaking words with hyphens. Setting type flush right, *rag left*, accomplishes the same thing:

_____

_____

_____

_____

_____

_____

_____

_____

Some layouts used *centered* type like this:

————————————————————

————————————————————————

————————————

——————————————————————

————————————————

——————————————————————

You can also choose to set type as a *run-around* to border an illustration. In this example the type runs around a picture of a guitar in order to emphasize its shape.

————————————————————

————————————————————

————————————————————

——————————————————

————————————————

——————————————————

————————————————————

————————————————————

————————————————

——————————————————

Now it's time to get started on your first rough layout.

Assignment

Take your idea for a campaign to sell Grand Tour Soups and make a full-page magazine ad. If you haven't got an idea of your own, use mine. But it will feel better if you give this assignment some thought and come up with something of your own that you can feel sure of and proud of.

Think it through visually. Make a list of visuals, including typographic elements, that you'll need. Diagram them, without drawing (except for designers), in some thumbnails until you've got what you like.

Now do it full size. During the course of this book, "full size" means a sheet of typing paper, or two sheets for a spread. This isn't exactly magazine page size, but it allows you to work with a copier, which will prove very important.

In this chapter you've learned how to reshape a classic layout, allowing it to evolve and grow from the idea. You've also learned how to indicate type.

New Key Terms

* justified
* rag left
* rag right
* run-around
* swipe
* thumbnail

CHAPTER 5

Learning Your ABCs

In this chapter you will

- learn how to trace type.

- learn how to letter better.

- understand type as a writer's tone of voice.

Some Important Basics

Even when you write long copy, you have to learn to think visually. Good writing looks good. Good copywriters learn what good typographic designers know: avoid long, solid blocks of copy.

Break copy up into shorter paragraphs. This is more inviting to the reader's eye and makes the copy look easy to read, not heavy and forbidding like a textbook on real estate law.

Now, it's time for you copy students to learn some new techniques that will improve the look of your "printing," which professionals call *lettering*. (Graphic design students might want to skip this section. It will look pretty simplistic.)

Copywriting students probably haven't given much thought to lettering for many years.

After learning to letter in kindergarten or the first grade, it was time to move on to more "grown-up" forms—the loops and strokes of writing—and a faster way to put words on paper. Well, now I want you to slow down. Don't do it faster; do it *better*.

You'll need:

- Some good writing instruments with a nice, comfortable feel. You'll probably want markers in several widths and some soft-tipped pens, fine, medium, and fat. Or soft lead pencils, if you like how they feel. *Don't* use a ballpoint. The thicker the stroke the better.

- Graph paper

- Tracing paper

- Masking tape

- A metal ruler, preferably with a cork backing to keep it from sliding

- *Some patience*

Remember that your writing and lettering habits have been established for many years. Learning to letter *better* may take some time. It may take a couple of hours—probably longer—but when you've got it, your writing is going to look better.

How to Make Words Look Better

For starters, I want you to trace an alphabet in all capital letters. Of course you already know how the letters look, but after you've traced them a couple of times, you'll learn and understand how the letters are formed. And how it *feels* when you form them right.

While there are hundreds of typefaces to choose from, they can generally be divided into two kinds: serif and sans serif (without serifs). To show you the difference, here's a letter with no serifs:

And here's one with serifs:

The serifs, the little cross lines at the tops and bottoms of the strokes, are vestiges of the medieval lettering done with a chisel-edged quill or reed pen.

To make your job easier, let's start tracing a sans serif alphabet. This classic type face, used often in advertising, is called Helvetica.

A B C D E F G H I

J K L M N O P Q

R S T U V W X Y Z

a b c d e f g h i j k l

m n o p q r s t u v

w x y z

Put a piece of tracing paper over the alphabet and hold it in place with some masking tape at the four corners. Now line up your ruler with the bottom of the first line of letters. This will keep your pen or marker from extending too far downwards. If you don't feel comfortable doing this, even with a cork-backed ruler, you may find it helpful to hold your ruler in place on the tracing paper with masking tape.

Trace the letters A,B,C,D, and E a couple of times. With these five letters, you've learned all the strokes you'll need for an alphabet. Vertical strokes, horizontal strokes, right and left diagonal strokes, and right and left curved strokes. It's as simple as that.

Now trace the rest of the alphabet, moving and, if necessary, taping down your ruler for each line. Now try it without taping the ruler in place. Trace the letters another time, or maybe two, until it feels easy and looks good.

The Freedom of Freehand

It's time to learn to letter without tracing. You'll still use tracing paper, but this time tape it on a sheet of graph paper. The lines will be your guide to the letter heights and vertical and horizontal lines.

Make your alphabet whatever height feels comfortable to you. The size you choose will depend on how thick your chosen writing instrument is. Letter the Helvetica alphabet that you've already traced a few times. If something doesn't look quite right, look at the letter on the alphabet page and remind yourself of how you made it.

After a couple of alphabets, you should be lettering with ease and confidence. You should *enjoy* doing it.

Remember, this isn't a grade school exercise or punishment for talking in class. You're improving your image, and you're learning how to give your ad its best shot.

Now it's time to try some words. Let's start by lettering something you've written a thousand times: your name. Using the tracing paper and ruler over the graph paper, write your name a few times. It probably looks pretty good, but something is missing, isn't it? You don't write your name in all capitals, but that's how you've lettered it. It's time to learn how to do lowercase letters.

The Ups and Downs of Type

Lowercase letter are not as easy to trace as capital letters because they add some new elements that your ruler won't like. These elements, called *descenders*, are the parts of the lowercase letters that hang down below the line of the body type. Not too many letter have descenders. Only these:

g j p q y

When you trace these letters use your ruler as a stop, just as you did with the capitalized alphabet. Ignore the descenders and just trace the body of the letters. When you're done, go back, move the ruler to where you want the descenders to line up, and add them.

Do that a few times, until you're ready to face the next set of hazards. They're called *ascenders*. Ascenders are the lines that go up higher than the body of the type. You'll find them only in these letters:

b d f h k l t

On the next page, you'll find a tracing-sized lowercase alphabet for practice.

Trace the lowercase alphabet a few times, just the way you did with the capitalized alphabet. This basic tracing should be easier to do by now. Then, use your graph paper to letter the alphabet without tracing. Finally, letter your name using both capitals and lowercase letters. Looks great, doesn't it? Of course you're not letter perfect yet. Like playing an instrument, it takes practice to improve your skills. But you've already learned how to read the music and how to play a scale, and that's a terrific start.

a b c d f g h i j

k l m n o p q r

s t u v w x y z

Assignment

Complete all the previous exercises.

For future exercises (and as a start in building your permanent reference file), the next few pages show some different alphabets you might want to learn. Some of them are thin, (called *light*), some are a bit thicker (called *medium*), and some are thick and heavy (called *bold.*)

There are serif and sans serif typefaces. Some are in Roman style, which means straight up and down, and some are in Italic style, which is slanted. There are also some stylized typefaces that can't easily be classified.

The reason there are so many letter forms and weights is that type not only communicates and ornaments, *type is a writer's tone of voice.* Therefore, every copywriter who cares about the craft must become knowledgeable about typography.

Bold type speaks strongly. Or it shouts.

Italics look urgent.

Some typefaces are very serious.

SOME ARE ROMANTIC.

Type faces with serifs somehow look more human and conversational than sans serif faces. Some typefaces communicate a particular period of time, like Colonial America or the 1880s or the 1930s, while some communicate a place, like France or England or Germany. Don't try to trace these alphabets. For now, just look them over to get a feel of what each communicates to you.

80 pt. Optima

ABCDEFGHI
JKLMNOPQR
STUVWXYZ
abcdefghijkl
mnopqrstuv
wxyz

80 pt. Futura Light

ABCDEFGHI
JKLMNOPQR
STUVWXYZ
abcdefghijkl
mnopqrstuv
wxyz

80 pt. Modula Roman

ABCDEFGHI

JKLMNOPQR

STUVWXYZ

abcdefghijkl

mnopqrstuv

wxyz

80 pt. Friz Quadrata

ABCDEFGHI

JKLMNOPQR

STUVWXYZ

abcdefghijkl

mnopqrstuv

wxyz

80 pt. Bauhaus Demi

ABCDEFGHI
JKLMNOPQR
STUVWXYZ
abcdefghijkl
mnopqrstuv
wxyz

80 pt. Gil Sans Light

ABCDEFGHI
JKLMNOPQR
STUVWXYZ
abcdefghijkl
mnopqrstuv
wxyz

80 pt. Times Roman

ABCDEFGH
IJKLMNOP
QRSTUVW
XYZ
abcdefghijkl
mnopqrstuv
wxyz

80 pt. Hiroshige Roman

ABCDEFGH
IJKLMNOP
QRSTUVW
XYZ

abcdefghijkl
mnopqrstuv
wxyz

80 pt. Bodoni 2

ABCDEFGHI
JKLMNOPQR
STUVWXYZ
abcdefghijkl
mnopqrstuv
wxyz
1234567890

80 pt. Lubalin Graph Demi

ABCDEFGH
IJKLMNOP
QRSTUVW
XYZ
abcdefghijk
lmnopqrstu
vwxyz

80 pt. Galliard

ABCDEFGH
IJKLMNOP
QRSTUVW
XYZ

abcdefghijkl
mnopqrstuv
wxyz

80 pt. New Century Schoolbook

ABCDEFG
HIJKLMNO
PQRSTUV
WXYZ

abcdefghijkl
mnopqrstuv
wxyz

80 pt. American Typewriter

ABCDEFGHI
JKLMNOPQR
STUVWXYZ
abcdefghijkl
mnopqrstuv
wxyz

80 pt. Zapf Chancery

ABCDEFGHI

JKLMNOPQR

STUVWXYZ

abcdefghijkl

mnopqrstuv

wxyz

80 pt. Dom Casual

ABCDEFGHI

JKLMNOPQR

STUVWXYZ

abcdefghijkl

mnopqrstuv

wxyz

80 pt. Bodega Roman

ABCDEFGHI
JKLMNOPQR
STUVWXYZ
abcdefghijkl
mnopqrstuv
wxyz

In this chapter you've learned how to trace type and how to letter without tracing. You've also learned to think of type as a writer's tone of voice.

★ ascenders

★ descenders

★ Roman

★ italic

★ serif

★ sans serif

Making Faces and Helping Hands

In this chapter you will

- make ovals happy, sad, surprised, and angry.
- learn a shortcut to drawing hands.
- put your first layout together.

Design students, feel free to take a break for the next few pages until you see the finished rough layout without words. Go out in the hall and snicker at how childish my drawings are. They are childish, I'll admit, but for rough layouts, they serve the purpose—to *communicate*.

Are you copywriters getting bored with all of those X-marked boxes where drawings should be? It's time to start learning how to draw.

Ovals Can Be Expressive

For the Grand Tour Parisian Onion Soup ad, the first thing you'll want to learn is how to make a face. Even more specifically, how to make the pleased and surprised face of a French chef.

For layout purposes, all faces look like this:

Here are quick and easy ways to give them a variety of expressions.

So far they're all neuter. To make one a man, a few strokes indicating hair will do.

To make a woman from one of the ovals, add curly hair.

Or add hair like this:

You can even give her some makeup:

Here's a blank oval that's big enough to trace and work with.

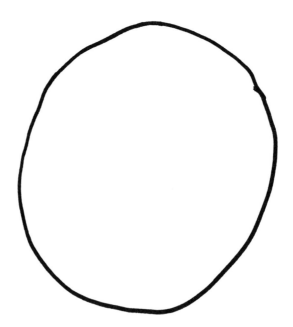

Assignment

Take a piece of tracing paper and hold it over the oval. Using your pencil, draw in a happy face.

If you don't like what you drew, move the tracing paper to a fresh place and try another happy face. Keep trying until you like what you've done. Then take a fresh piece of tracing paper and use your black marker to trace your pencil drawing.

You now have a usable piece of "art" (that's what it's called in the trade) that can be put into a layout by making a succession of tracings. Before we get to that step, however, do some more exercises with the blank oval face.

Assignment

Trace the oval. Then, don't trace, but copy some of the expressions I made for you, just to get the feel of how they were done. Play around with them for fifteen minutes or so and you'll see how easy and fun they are to do.

Now let's get to that French chef. I showed you how to do a happy face and how to do a surprised face. Now all you have to do is to combine these expressions on one face. *Do these drawing exercises as you read.*

Draw the smile of the happy face. Then, add the raised eyebrows of the surprised face, like this:

That works, but it hasn't got much character. Let's see what he looks like if we tilt his mouth to one side a little and give him a small mustache. The little waxed mustache is an old convention that will help make him look "French."

Now all he needs is a chef's hat. A chef's hat is shaped sort of like a mushroom, with the top of the mushroom softly crushed. Try a few chef's hats on tracing paper held over this face. When you've got one that looks okay, try moving the tracing paper to set the hat at different angles.

When you've got it the way you like it, use some pieces of masking tape to secure the tracing paper with the hat to the tracing paper with the face. Finally, put down a fresh piece of tracing paper over both drawings and with your soft pencil trace the complete face with the chef's hat on it. When that's done to your satisfaction, carefully go over your pencil lines with black marker lines. Then use your kneaded eraser to get rid of the pencil lines.

Viola! You've created a French chef, your "art" for the Grand Tour Soup ad. And *you* drew it!

I don't need to teach you how to draw a bowl of soup or a can. It's as easy as this:

The bowl consists of just an oval and an arc. The two wavy lines over the bowl are a standard way to indicate steam.

Drawing Hands That Aren't All Thumbs

Now, to finish the drawing of the French chef, you'll need to give him a spoon of soup and a hand to hold it. It might be nice if his other hand was giving an okay sign, with the forefinger and thumb touching and the other fingers straight up.

Hands are hard to do right, but everybody knows that, so you won't get any criticism for klutzy hands. Fortunately, there's an easy and acceptable shorthand form you can use to draw hands.

Assignment

To begin, if you're right-handed, look carefully at your own left hand. That's your model. If you're a lefty, your right hand is your model.

Hands in use almost never look like tracings of flat hands.

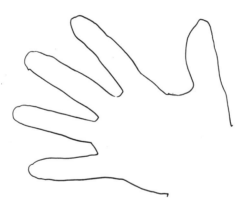

Hands mostly occupy a round space, like a ball, with a projection that's the thumb. Like this:

Now see how easy it is to add fingers to that shape, if you need them. I have drawn a hand that can hold a spoon, but it doesn't even need fingers.

Let me show you a few variations you can make just by "rotating" the round shape, with and without fingers:

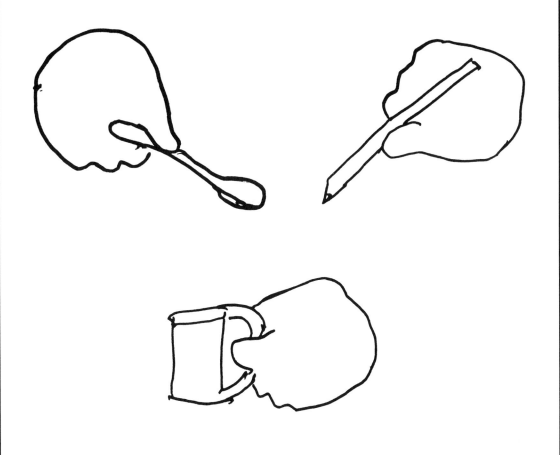

I know that none of my drawings really looks like a hand, but I'm certain you understand what each hand is doing, and that's all you'll need to communicate in a rough layout. Remember, you're learning how to *communicate visually* not how to make fine illustrations.

For the French chef, draw something similar to the hand with a spoon and the "okay" hand sign. Make the drawings whatever size you want. They should be a little less than half the size of the face. If you don't like what you've drawn, trace over it to make it better. Then, trace over your second drawing to make it better. Keep tracing until it looks good enough. With hands, good enough is good enough.

Putting the Layout Together

Now you have all the visual elements you'll need for your soup ad:

- A French chef enjoying soup

- One of his hands holding a spoon of soup

- His other hand making an okay sign

- A bowl of soup and a can

- A headline

- A subhead

- A small block of copy

It's time to put all of these elements together, not in a thumbnail, but in a full-size magazine page layout.

Assignment

Assemble a rough layout by following the steps outlined below.

On a fresh piece of tracing paper, use your soft black marker pen to trace the outline of a piece of typing paper. You won't draw on this outline tracing; instead you'll draw on another piece of tracing paper that is laid over it. This method will let you throw out your drawing and start over without having to measure the page again. Now you'll just place a fresh sheet of tracing paper over the guide.

Your first step in preparing the layout will be to use your pencil and ruler to divide the page into areas, one for each of the main visual elements.

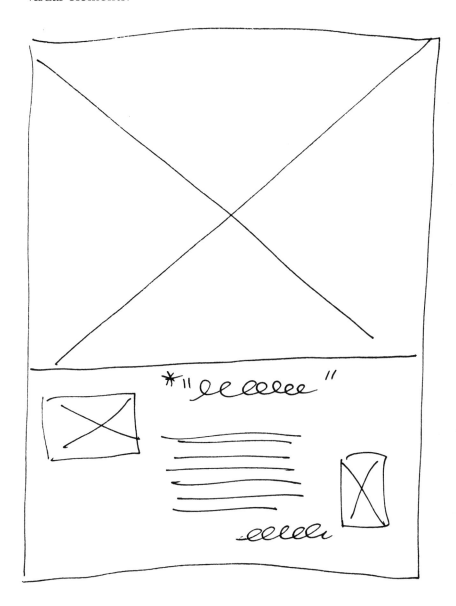

Now, using a separate piece of tracing paper, make an oval for the chef's face. Start drawing, tracing, and assembling the face and the chef's hat, as you did before, until the French chef is drawn to size, the way you want him.

Next, use the same steps with the soup bowl. Draw the bowl to a size that will fit in its box. Once you've appropriately sized the bowl, you can decide whether you want to present the bowl of soup literally in a drawn, outlined box or out in the open. My personal preference is not to box the bowl in, but the final decision is yours.

On yet another piece of tracing paper, draw a can the size you want.

Now it's time to assemble all of these visuals into one layout. This is really simple. Just trace each of your pictures on a fresh piece of tracing paper and tape it over the page outline in its appropriate position.

Now, on still another fresh piece of tracing paper, make loops or V's to indicate the headline that is to go over the chef's head. Make the headline the size you want, and then put it under your main layout paper and move it around until it's where you want it. Now, trace the headline indicator onto the layout.

Repeat the same for the subhead and the copy.

Look at what you've got. Even without words, you've got a rough layout that *communicates*. Anyone who gives the page more than a passing glance will know that this is an ad for a good tasting, authentically French, canned soup. Think how effective your ad will be with the right words!

Explore the Cosmos of Possibilities

This layout grew from the idea, exactly the way it was supposed to, but it's not the one and only inevitable layout. There are endless possibilities for you to try. Create some different rough layouts in thumbnail size. You might use some of the standard layouts that I showed you. Or, since this isn't the real world yet and nothing you can do is wrong, break the rule about not acting like a designer. Make a layout all your own, for your very own Grand Tour Soup ad. If it's a stinker, who'll know but you?

Assignment

Before going on to the next chapter, practice making faces with different expressions. Go back to the page of faces I drew for you and try to draw them without tracing. It's not hard to do. Draw each face a few times until you feel you can do it without looking at my examples.

Practice indicating headlines with loopy strokes. Use your ruler and your marker to draw two guide lines, one for the top of the loops and one for the bottom.

Put a piece of tracing paper over the guidelines. Now, use your marker to make sequences of loops between the guidelines. Have some words in mind, such as "I feel idiotic making loops instead of lettering words." That way your loops will appear to be short and long words. Loosen up and do it for a while until you are comfortable making your loops in straight lines.

Do the same thing with angular, V-shaped strokes. Use your ruler to stop the downstroke of your marker, and use the upper guideline to keep the top points of your V's lined up. Be sure to break the strokes into word-sized groupings, the way you did with the loops.

In this chapter you've learned how to indicate faces and give them different expressions, how to draw a hand in action, and how to assemble a layout.

✳   art

CHAPTER 7

Bodies to Put Your Hands On

In this chapter you will learn

- how to use triangles to build bodies.
- how stick figures help create motion.
- how to use your own experience to make ads.

You Are a Triangle

Now we are going to learn how to draw bodies for your faces and hands. Start by taking a look at your own body in a full length mirror. Look at your torso, your arms, and your legs. What do you see? Not sticks. What you see are triangles. Of course, they are rounded and may look more like ovals to you, but underneath they are triangles—long triangles, full triangles, and thin triangles.

The torso is a fairly full triangle, like this:

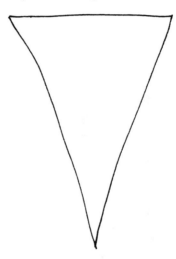

The arms are made of two triangles, a thin one and a thinner one.
They're attached to the torso triangle like this:

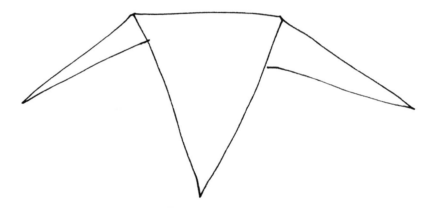

Overlapping the bottom of the torso triangle is a pelvic triangle.

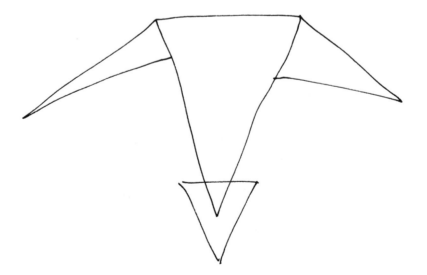

The legs are attached to the pelvic triangle. Draw a long, slightly slim thigh triangle, attach a thinner triangle, and add two flattened triangles for feet.

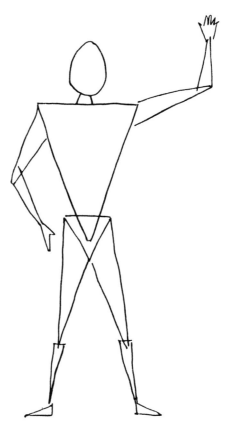

It looks pretty silly, doesn't it? Those triangles are just diagrams. Now they need some softness, some rounding, to make them look more human.

Triangle Man Meets Triangle Woman

Put a sheet of tracing paper over Triangle Man. Think about what you must do to feminize these triangles. You may want to narrow the shoulders and widen the hips a little. Modify the drawing a few times until you like what you've got. Use your soft pencil to round out and fill in the obvious places. Sketch lightly, and go over your lines as often as you like.

If some part of the figure starts looking too fat, slim it down with your kneaded eraser. When you've got a line you like, pencil it firmly and darkly over the light sketch strokes. Keep working until the whole figure looks okay. Now, take another sheet of tracing paper and use your soft-tipped pen to trace the dark lines.

Stick with It

Now it's time to put your figure into motion. Believe it or not, this is the easiest part, because it starts with something you've probably been drawing since you were a little kid—a stick figure.

Here's a familiar stick figure, running.

Draw a stick figure of your own and then put a sheet of tracing paper over it and sketch in the triangles, like this:

Now, modify that drawing to make it look more human.

Here are a bunch of stick figures doing some of the things you might want to illustrate in your ads: sitting, lying down, eating and drinking, working at a desk, walking, and skiing.

Practice drawing these figures.

Most figures are really easy to draw. The hard things are often the inanimate objects associated with the figures. For example, it's a snap to draw a stick figure that will ride a bike.

But drawing a bike is harder than assembling a real one. If you need to draw a stick figure on a bike, find a bike photo in a magazine or in a catalog, trace it, and then draw a stick figure riding it.

You can save yourself a lot of headaches by starting to build your swipe file now. Get into the habit of cutting out pictures of people doing things, plus pictures of objects, room scenes, buildings, pieces of furniture, bottles, glasses, cars, boats, landscapes, and so on.

Use Your Experience

You know what interests you, and you'll make the best ads when you create them for things about which you have some interest and some knowledge. It is wise to build your swipe file with that fact in mind. If you like to ski, for example, you'll do well to create ads for ski equipment and ski resorts. So, collect pictures of skis, boots, people skiing, people on ski lifts, snowy mountain scenes, ski lodge lounging areas with cozy fireplaces, etc.

Always try to create ads for things you know something about. That doesn't mean you have to be an expert. Just being an experienced consumer will do fine. That way, you'll know how other consumers make decisions.

You probably know a lot more things than you think, even if they are things you *don't* know. For example, if you don't know how to cook, you *do* know how to eat without cooking. With that knowledge, you can do ads for Burger King, Pizza Hut, or for Kraft Macaroni & Cheese. You might do an ad for a line of frozen dinners, a brand of bread, cold cuts, mustard, mayonnaise, or a microwave oven. Cut out pictures that relate to these things and add them to your swipe file. Then, work out an ad for food.

Assignment

Taco Bell is hampered by its name. The national chain hasn't even tried to get into the profitable breakfast business. Your client, a regional association of Taco Bell franchise owners, wants to try. They want to tell consumers that Mexican traditional breakfast specialties are delicious. The ad will feature Ranch Style Eggs. These are fried eggs on a white flour tortilla, topped with melted cheese and salsa.

Create a black-and-white newspaper ad introducing Ranch Style Eggs and mentioning the availability of other, more familiar breakfast dishes.

Caution: don't use a photograph of the featured food for appetite appeal. It will look awful in black-and-white. You'll have to find some other way to get people interested in trying Taco Bell's Ranch Style Eggs for breakfast.

In this chapter you've learned how to build bodies from triangles and how to put them in motion. You've also learned to trust your own experience in building a swipe file.

Part Three

Putting Words Into Action

CHAPTER 8

Time to Start Writing

In this chapter you will learn

● how the headline affects the layout.

● to think your way through a long copy ad.

● "casting" for a written tone of voice.

The Headline

Have you figured out yet what you'd like the French chef to say? There are many possibilities, including:

"Someone stole my onion soup recipe!"

"This onion soup is from a can? Impossible!"

"I will never make onion soup again."

And so on. What would *you* like him to say? Or, more to the point, what would you like the *headline* to say? Just because I thought the headline might be good as a quote from the chef doesn't mean that this is the only way, or even the best way, to go.

Try writing a few headlines of your own. If you think they need subheads, write them, too. Forget that you showed a subhead on the first right layout that you drew, because that can always be changed. Remember: *let the layout grow from the idea*. For example, if you'd like a headline that says, "How we talked Chef Armand LaTour out of his famous onion soup recipe," you'll be developing a completely different look from the one we just put together.

How the Headline Affects the Layout

The "How we talked. . ." headline promises to tell a story, and that means you'll want a layout that allows for fairly long copy. If you still want to show the chef, you'll probably want to show him with some expression other than pleased surprise and you may want to give up on an appetizing shot of a bowl of soup. If that's the ad you want to do, then go ahead and do it. Here's how to go about it.

A Short Course in Long Copy

Start by rereading the positioning statement and the advertising strategy for Grand Tour Soups. Before you rush to your typewriter, word processor, or paper and pencils, you need some guidance in writing long copy.

First of all, relax. Long copy is easier to write than short copy. Short copy often requires a diamond cutter's accuracy and nerve. Long copy gives you time to develop a story, pause for effect, digress a bit, and amble comfortably to a conclusion.

The Cast

Before you start writing, I want you to do something that will sound a little odd. I want you to "cast," as if the ad was meant to be read aloud by an actor. This will give your copy a singular tone of voice that can be a signature for your client.

The Voice

Ask yourself who the writer should be. Start by deciding whether the writer is a man or woman, what age he or she is, and what level of education he or she has attained. Decide whether your writer is urban or rural, has a foreign or regional accent, or has any additional distinguishing characteristics that can help define the character.

If you like, think of an actor who would be appropriate as a spokesperson. If you select a Whoopie Goldberg sort of woman, you'll write in a very different style than you will if you cast a Harrison Ford sort of man.

When you've settled on your character, look again at our initial headline idea: "How we talked Chef Armand LaTour out of his famous onion soup recipe." Does this work for your character? Maybe the corporate "we" is no longer appropriate. Would it be better if the headline read: "How I. . ."? That simple change would give you a completely different piece of copy from the "we" version. It would also change the picture, because, as it stands, the writer will appear to be another French chef.

I think the "I" version, though very inviting, creates more problems than it solves, so let's stick with the "we." If your character isn't comfortable with the corporate "we," you had better start to cast again.

Subheads and Lead-Ins

Now that you've settled on the headline and the tone of voice for your copy, consider the use of a subhead or a short paragraph of boldfaced lead-in copy. These approaches allow you to encapsulate your message up front and minimize the risk of losing your reader before the finish of the long copy.

For example, I wrote, *"One of many tales of international intrigue behind authentically delicious Grand Tour Soups."* This lead-in communicates everything you really want to say in a few words. It also promises an interesting story. Note that it is not in any "character" tone of voice but in an impersonal editorial style. You can follow this type of lead-in with any storytelling style you might want.

Crossheads

If you're planning to write 150 to 250 words (anything longer than that is probably too long) plan to break up your copy with crossheads. Crossheads are brief headlines, usually set in bold type just a little larger than the body copy. Crossheads serve three purposes:

1. They make the page more inviting to read. A solid block of copy can look forbidding to many readers.

2. They allow the reader a brief rest as well as an invitation to read on.

3. They allow the reader the option of getting the story while skipping as much of the copy as desired.

This means that you must plan your crossheads to make your key selling points in a sequential, logical way. This doesn't mean that your crossheads should be dull and pedestrian. On the contrary, they should be presented in the character tone of voice you've selected and should spark the copy.

Body Copy

In actually writing the body copy, I suggest that you loosen up and write as freely as you want, not pausing to count or estimate the number of words you've used. Just tell the story, making it as interesting, informative, and as full of selling points as you can. When you've done this, and after you've revised and rewritten it a few times, it is time to make the words fit the layout.

Cutting

If the ad is too long, start cutting. You'll be amazed at how many words you can get rid of in a piece of copy without losing anything important. In fact, you'll find that cutting will actually improve your writing. Bob Levenson, a member of the Copywriter's Hall of Fame, likes to say, "I don't think I'm a terrific writer. But, boy, can I cut."

The best lesson in cutting that I know comes from Sir Arthur Quiller-Couch, in "The Art of Writing." He counseled, "Murder your darlings." Quiller-Couch was not speaking only of cutting. He meant *always* murder your darlings, not only to shorten what you've written. If you've come up with a phrase or a sentence that you think is just brilliant, get rid of it first. If you don't, that phrase will always stick out and call attention to itself (and brilliant you) and will distract attention from your message. I don't know of a more difficult rule to observe or a more perilous one to ignore.

Why Write Long Copy Ads?

You may wonder whether it's ever a good idea to write a long copy ad in a society pressured by so many demands on time and energy. Why write long copy at all, when you must also write crossheads that will allow readers to skip it?

Go back again to the strategy. Your target is college-educated men and women. This group will probably like the idea that an advertiser is treating them as intelligent people, even if they don't actually read the whole ad. Getting your target reader to like the advertiser (as opposed to the advertising) is the first step towards a sale.

There's another reason for long copy, given the appropriate product. When I worked for Ogilvy & Mather, I knew that people were buying Mercedes automobiles mainly as status symbols. I asked David Ogilvy whether he really thought these people would read the more than 400 words in the agency's Mercedes ads. He said he was sure they would not, but the sheer presence of so much copy was in itself a message. "It says there's a lot to be said for this car."

Now let's get back to creating a campaign for Grand Tour Soups. You may like the long copy version, or you may prefer another approach. If so, work on that idea. I'll just move ahead with what I want to do, and you can follow along and see if you learn anything that can be put to use in your ad.

I've decided on my headline, which will be the same in every ad. (This is called a "standing headline.") It will read:

"Only in America!"

Each time the headline appears, it will be shown in the language of the chef being portrayed. In this instance, it will read:

"Seulement en Etats Unis!"✼

The big, bold asterisk will refer to the subhead:

✼"Only in America!"

The short copy will say that you can't get canned Parisian Onion Soup this authentic and this good anywhere, even in France. It will mention that there are serving suggestions on the label, and it will name a few other Grand Tour soups. The rest of the ads in this campaign will practically write themselves.

Now take the time you need to think through and create your own campaign.

In this chapter you've learned how different headlines will lead you to different visuals and different layouts, how to construct a long copy ad, and how to use subheads, bold leads, and crossheads.

New Key Terms

✶ lead-ins

✶ crosshead

✶ body copy

Life After Layouts

In this chapter you will

● learn how to turn a layout into an ad.

● understand the need for an art director.

● meet the specialists, photographers, and engravers.

● travel through the print production track.

Before leaving print advertising, you should know what it takes to turn a layout into a finished ad in a magazine or newspaper. If you're a copywriter, you'll need an art director to help you.

About Art Directors

First, the ad's elements must be created. Your art director selects a photographer or two if necessary and has the final say on location or set, casting, wardrobe, and props. Later, the art director specifies the type, supervises any needed photo retouching, and gives final approval of engraving and proofs that are to be sent to magazines.

If you're a copywriter and you have no art director with whom to work, your first step is to visit the art and design studios in your town and size up the quality of their work. Pick a studio where you feel good personal chemistry and see work you like.

About Photographers

For my Grand Tour Soup ad I'll need photographs of a French chef, a bowl of soup, and a can of soup. The art director selects a photographer who's good at shooting people and another who specializes in shots of products and food. Very few photographers can do both well.

Food and package photographers are a special breed, and their speciality is called "tabletop." If your tabletop photographer is good, he or she will do more than take pictures. Good photographers have ideas of their own that may improve the communication and change the look of the ad.

For example, the photographer who specializes in people might suggest that shooting the chef in limbo (that's what a blank background is called) might not only be a little dull, but it might actually be misleading as well. What's to make the reader think that this chef is in Paris and not just working in a French restaurant in St. Louis or Omaha?

Wouldn't it work better, he might suggest, and also be a lot more interesting to look at, if we were to shoot him in the kitchen of an old and atmospheric French restaurant? Don't say no too fast. Even though you and your client are happy with the ad as it is conceived, think it over. Remember that your rough layout was only a way of communicating an idea. Don't pass up a chance to make it work better.

The tabletop photographer may make a good contribution, too. He might suggest that the bowl of soup would look more interesting and appetizing if he were to shoot it on a red-and-white-checked placemat with some French bread, a glass of wine, and a napkin.

Consider both of these suggestions. If you like the kitchen location idea, find out how much more it will cost to shoot than if done in limbo. Must the photographer go to France? Can he have a convincing one-wall set built in his studio? Or can he find a good French kitchen location in Quebec or Montreal? Talk it over with your client and move forward with whatever you agree to do.

The photographer who specializes in people does some location search in Canada (if that's what you and your client agreed on), does some casting, and takes a few test shots. The art director and you then select the location and model you like best.

The Mechanical Starts with Type

Meanwhile, the art director (or, in a larger design studio or ad agency, the type director) specifies the type and has it set by a typography house. In a small agency, or a well-equipped studio, the type will probably be set in-house on a computer.

Using rubber cement, the type is then secured in place on a piece of white cardboard that is ruled to the exact size of the space the ad is to occupy.

The Photos Come Next

When the photos come in, they are photostated in exactly the size that will appear in the ad. The stats are then pasted in position on the white board. Since they're not "art," which means they are not intended for reproduction, the stats are marked "for position only," or FPO.

If the type is to be printed over the art, the way my headline overlaps the chef's hat, the headline type is pasted on a clear acetate sheet and positioned over the "position only" photostat. The finished result is called a *mechanical*.

Print Production Track

The mechanical and the art (the color photo) are then sent to an engraver, who photographs the *line elements* (in this case, the type) and the *halftone elements* (the photo).

Unlike a photo or a painting, where the color is continuous, printed photos are all one shade. In a black-and-white printed photo, there are no grays. Everything is black dots or white paper, and the gray shades are achieved by varying dot size and the distance between dots. If you look closely at a photo in a newspaper using a magnifying glass you'll see what I mean. It's not hard to see in this medium, because newspaper photography is pretty coarse, usually using only 65 lines of dots per inch each way. It is harder to see the dots in magazine color halftones because they are usually screened as fine as 133 lines each way per inch. By comparison, fine art reproduction may have as many as 300 lines of dots each way per inch.

Using a process that's too complex to go into here, the engraver separates the color photos into four halftone engraving plates. One plate is for the black ink, which is used for line art (headline and copy) that will not be screened and for screened photographs that will need some black ink in the mix. The other three plates are for the blue, yellow, and red tones of the photos. When all four plates are printed on top of each other in precise alignment (called perfect *register*), the result is a complete four-color *proof* of the ad. If the output looks too red, too blue, or too yellow, your art director or print production specialist works with the engraver to make adjustments to the offending plate, or *separation*.

When everyone has approved the final proof, it is sent, with the plates, to the magazine in which it is to appear. The proof serves as the magazine printer's guide for reproducing the color.

For a black-and-white ad, the same process is followed. The engraver shoots the line art and then, using photographic screens, shoots the photos to render them as a series of dots. He then assembles both line and halftone elements on a single plate to be sent, with a proof, to the newspaper.

That's a summary of the print production track. Supervising and controlling this process is primarily the art director's job, but there is one place where the copywriter is needed, and that is during the proofreading stage.

Proofreading

After the type has been set, you will receive proofs of it. It is your job to see that the type is correct and that it reads right. Of course you'll want to compare the proof with your final copy to see that there are no words left out, set in the wrong order, or simply misspelled.

The copy should also be checked for sense and appearance; for example, bad word breaks should be corrected and lines of copy that are just too short (called *widows*) should be eliminated. To get the type to look right, you may want to cut or add a word or two or reconfigure your paragraphs.

When correcting proofs, you should always use standard proof-reader's marks, which let you communicate professionally with the typographer. Here, for future reference, are all the proofreader's marks you will ever use, plus a few your printer has probably never seen.

∧	Make correction indicated in margin.	⌐¬	Raise to proper position.
Stet	Retain crossed-out word or letter; let it stand.	⌐¬	Lower to proper position.
		////	Hair space letters.
. . . . *Stet*	Retain words under which dots appear; write "Stet" in margin.	*w.f.*	Wrong font; change to proper font.
		Qu?	Is this right?
✗	Appears battered; examine.	*l.c.*	Put in lower case (small letters).
≡	Straighten lines.	*s.c.*	Put in small capitals.
⋁⋁⋁	Unevenly spaced; correct spacing.	*Caps*	Put in capitals.
//	Line up; i.e., make lines even with other matter.	*C.&s.c.*	Put in caps and small caps.
		rom.	Change to roman.
run in	Make no break in the reading; no ¶	*ital.*	Change to italic.
no ¶	No paragraph; sometimes written "run in."	≡	Under letter or word means caps.
		=	Under letter or word, small caps.
out see copy	Here is an omission; see copy.	—	Under letter or word means italic.
¶	Make a paragraph here.	∼∼∼	Under letter or word, bold face.
tr	Transpose words or letters as indicated.	⸲/	Insert comma.
ℐ	Take out matter indicated; dele.	⸵/	Insert semicolon.
ℐ̱	Take out character indicated and close up.	⸲/	Insert colon.
¢	Line drawn through a cap means lower case.	⊙	Insert period.
		/?/	Insert interrogation mark.
℗	Upside down; reverse.	(!)	Insert exclamation mark.
⌣	Close up; no space.	/=/	Insert hyphen.
#	Insert a space here.	⸲ᵛ	Insert apostrophe.
⊥	Push down this space.	⸲ᵛ⸲ᵛ	Insert quotation marks.
□	Indent line one em.	℮/	Insert superior letter or figure.
⌐	Move this to the left.	⌐|	Insert inferior letter or figure.
⌐	Move this to the right.	[/]	Insert brackets.
		(/)	Insert parentheses.
		⅟m	One-em dash.
		⅟m	Two-em parallel dash.

In this chapter you've learned what an art director does. You have also learned how to turn a layout into an ad with the help of specialists such as photographers and photoengravers. Most important, you've toured the length of the advertising print production track.

* halftone art

* limbo

* line art

* mechanical

* plates

* print production track

* proof

* register

* separation

* tabletop

* widow

Part Four

Creating Reality from Thin Air

CHAPTER 10

The Theater of the Mind

In this chapter you will

- understand why radio is the most visual medium of all.

- gain insight into the power of sound effects, music, and the human voice.

- learn how to time a radio commercial.

I know you're dying to get to work on TV, but you are not ready for that just yet. You've got a little more work to do in learning to think visually. You need to explore the extraordinary visual aids called sound effects, music, and voices.

We are now going to learn about radio, the most visual medium of all. When you listen to radio, the pictures are your own creation. You make them in your own mind, with just a little help from the writer and producer. It is the energy of your imagination that makes radio so powerful.

Art directors, don't skip this section! You may never actually write a radio spot, but I'm sure you want to become a creative director someday, and you'll have to know about radio. Also, learning to think visually in radio will help you when it's time to start your first TV commercial.

Radio's Often Overlooked Power

Most radio commercials I hear today take little, if any, advantage of the medium's visual possibilities. Maybe that's because the people who write them nowadays weren't raised as I was, in the days of radio plays.

Today you often hear radio commercials in the form of dialogs between two people. Most of these radio spots are visually blind. They don't even give you a clue about *who* and *where* these people are. These added dimensions can make a radio commercial more real and are quite easy to develop.

SFX: EEEE—BLOOP!

In a famous commercial for the Radio Ad Council, copywriter and comic Stan Freberg told us that Lake Michigan had been drained and filled with hot chocolate. He then pushed a 700-foot mountain of whipped cream into it. The sound effects (SFX) included the groaning and creaking of the mountain leading to a big splash. Then, he cued the Royal Canadian Air Force to fly overhead with a ten ton maraschino cherry and drop it into the whipped cream (SFX: bomblike whistle and bloop!), all to the cheering of 25,000 extras.

The sound effects and urgent commentary made this image perfectly real, completely visual. Having made us *see* this happen, Freberg concluded triumphantly, "Now . . . you wanta try that on television?"

Are You Hearing Voices?

You should be, because your first great visual aid in radio is the human voice. Never start writing a radio spot until you have done some casting in your mind. Who's going to do the talking? A man? A woman? What kind of man or woman? Young? Middle-aged? Old? Urban? Rural? Working class? Middle class? Upper class? White? Black? Will the speaker have a foreign accent or an American regional accent? And what will this person's attitude be? Warm and friendly? Urgent? Authoritative? Amusing? Amused? Angry? Cautionary? Seductive? Newsy?

A Place for Everything

Next, ask yourself, where is this person? A sense of place can do wonders for your writing. Here's a simple example taken from an old Pepperidge Farm radio commercial.

You hear some up-close sounds of hammering. (The effect of up-close is achieved by a moderately loud sound level.) In the far distance (much lower sound level) are barnyard effects—chickens, a cow, and some chirping birds. Then, in the mid-distance (medium–low volume), a woman shouts: "Henry! What're you doin' on that roof?"

It's as simple as that. You not only know something about who those people are, as well as where they are, but you even have a *camera angle*. Because you hear the hammering nearby with the barnyard sounds in the background and the woman in the mid-distance, you, as a "viewer," are on that roof with Henry, looking down. It's almost dizzying, and yet it was done with nothing more than a good mix of audio levels, plus stock sound effects that are available in any audio studio.

If all you want is the "white space" background a studio gives you, that's okay, but it is not a given. It is a choice you must make. You could choose to use standard sound effects to put your talker almost anywhere—on a city street, in a porch rocker on a summer evening, in a restaurant, at a party, or on a beach in the Caribbean. How can you let us know those lapping waves are in the Caribbean and not California or Spain? You use your final great radio visual aid: *music*.

The Music of Places

A steel band playing "Yellow Bird" in the background sure can't be California or Spain. Ukuleles and steel guitars will instantly transport that beach to Hawaii. Mandolins will put it in Italy. Spain can be conjured up with Flamenco guitars and clacking castanets. Mexico can be created with a mariachi brass-and-string band.

So, even a simple "talking head" radio spot can be made much more interesting by being specific about who is talking and by creating a staged place and developing its atmosphere.

The Music of Time

Your choice of sound effects and music can even put your announcer in a different time than today, because few things are more readily dated than music. The Sixties don't sound like today, the Forties don't sound like the Sixties, and the Twenties don't sound like the Forties.

Don't Get Carried Away

Careful sound selection can put your announcer at a ball in Mozart's Vienna or at a cowboy saloon in frontier America. This is terrific freedom, but like all freedoms, it's a little dangerous if it's misused.

Be sure that your casting, location, time, and mood are all *relevant to what you're selling*. Don't let yourself get carried away by the fun of creating unless it makes it easier for the listener to understand and remember your message.

Plan Your Radio Spot

Plan a commercial for the Grand Tour Parisian Onion Soup campaign and make it work in a way that's consistent with your print campaign. Don't start writing until you've done your visualizing and planning.

Settle on the Idea

Here are some possible considerations:

- You can use one or more voices, SFX, and music that suggests Paris (an accordion usually does the job).

- You could start in Paris and stay there.

- You could start in Paris and end in the U.S.

- You could start in the U.S., visit Paris, and either stay there or come home.

- You could come home to the deep South, to the Maine coast, or to a young couple's apartment in a city.

- You could use a sound studio with a neutral American voice.

- You could have an announcer make the key selling points, or you could weave them into a dialog.

Whatever you choose to do, it should now be clear that you must first, just as you did in print advertising, visualize your radio commercial. Then, you can start to write it.

Choose Your Length

In addition to your other choices, you have a choice of how long the commercial will be. In radio it's still possible to have sixty seconds, provided your client wants to pay for it. If you think that a 60-second spot would slow things down too much and that you can make your points better in a shorter form, write a 30-second commercial.

Timing Tips

Here are some useful tips about timing your commercial:

- Buy an inexpensive stop watch. It will be a basic working tool during your whole life in advertising.

- Unless you want an urgent, rapid-fire harangue, almost any professional announcer will speak much slower than you will when you read your copy aloud.

- The announcer needs the time to give character to the spot and to emphasize the key selling points.

- A good rule of thumb is to make your own timed reading at least 15 percent shorter than the spot.

- Figure on no more than 50 seconds of your reading for a 60-second spot and 23 seconds for a 30-second spot.

- If you want to use music, write at least 6 seconds less talk in a :60 and 4 seconds less in a :30. This allows you to "open up" the talk in order to hear the music "in the clear" once or twice, rather than just using it as a barely audible "bed," way below the voice level.

- If you include SFX, be sure to time them. Remember that not all SFX are created equal. For example, if you expect a listener to understand that a faint hooting sound is a distant train whistle, it will take a minimum of three seconds to be clear. By comparison, a two-chime doorbell will be obvious in only one and a quarter seconds.

Okay. You're ready to visualize your radio spot. Enjoy it. If you don't, neither will your listeners.

Time to Write some Radio

To help you write radio scripts, here's a format sample that is also a fine example of the use of SFX. Note that the script supplies brief casting specs and some limited directions.

:60 Radio
American Heart Association
"Heart Attack Sounds"

SFX:	HEARTBEATS UP, THEN UNDER
ANNC'R:	(MALE, NEUTRAL AMERICAN ACCENT) This is how a heart attack kills you. Your arteries start out very smooth on the inside...
SFX:	SMOOTH SYNTHESIZED SOUNDS REPRESENTING ARTERIES WORKS WITH THE HEARTBEATS.
ANNC'R:	...and your blood courses freely through them, pumped by your heart.
SFX:	ADD SOUNDS LIKE BLOOD COURSING
ANNC'R:	You've heard about cholesterol.
SFX:	DISSONANT, THICK CHOLESTEROL SOUNDS ARE ADDED AND BUILD.
ANNC'R:	Cholerterol comes from many of the foods we eat. Too much of it in your blood can slowly build up to line your arteries. This buildup is called plaque, and it narrows the openings, making it hard for your blood to pass through. This would be bad enough, but there's something else about plaque. It's rough.
SFX:	ROUGH TEARING SOUNDS ARE ADDED. THE INTERWOVEN SOUNDS START BUILDING TO A CRESCENDO.
ANNC'R:	(AGITATED) Your blood is designed to clot when it hits a foreign substance.
SFX:	"CLOTTING" SOUNDS, THE LOUDEST YET, ARE ADDED.
ANNC'R:	(MORE AND MORE AGITATED) Not recognizing the rough surfaces, a clot forms, blocking the narrowed artery that feeds your heart. Oxygen is cut off, and your heart chokes.
SFX:	SOUNDS BUILD TO A FRENZY

ANNC'R: . . . and then you die.

SFX: TOTAL SILENCE FOR A MOMENT, THEN REGU-
LAR HEARTBEAT SOUND BEGINS AGAIN.

ANNC'R: (CALM AGAIN) You can prevent heart disease. We can
tell you how. Call your American Heart Association.

Assignment

Write a 60-second spot for Grand Tour Soups
Write a 30-second spot for Grand Tour Soups
Write a :30 and a :60 for any two products or services of
your choice.

Be sure to time your commercials and to note the time on
the script. Note your actual reading time and your estimate of the
professional reading time. Also note the time given to SFX and music
"in the clear."

In this chapter you've learned why radio is the
most visual medium of all. You've gained insight into the power of
sound effects, music, and the human voice, and you've learned to
plan and time a radio commercial.

New Key Terms

✳ SFX

✳ music bed

✳ in the clear

CHAPTER 11

TV: Show Business Is All Business

In this chapter you will

- learn what a storyboard is and how it's used.

- understand what a scene is.

- see what a frame is and why it's not a unit of time.

- study different kinds of storyboards, including the Key Frame, the Working Board, and the Shooting Board.

- learn how to create a Key Frame Board and a Working Storyboard.

- think your way through a storyboard.

- learn to write in storyboard language and abbreviations.

- be introduced to and learn how to indicate titles, supers, mortises, tags, dissolves, wipes, and other opticals.

- understand how music can intensify, or even change, the meaning of what the audience sees.

TV Has It All

TV has motion, actors performing and speaking on screen, unseen voices, color, music, dance, SFX, animation, graphics, type and lettering, illustration, still photos, special effects—you name it.

It's safe to say, with today's technology in film, tape, and computers, that there's nothing you can dream up in your wildest fantasy that you can't make happen on the screen. The only limitation is money.

In TV, Money Is the Medium

In my experience, often working with budgets of hundreds of thousands of dollars to produce a 30-second spot, I've always felt the limitations of money. I've never spent a dollar the effect of which couldn't be seen or heard in the commercial. And when budgets were tight, I've never saved a dollar that didn't leave a flaw in the commercial that would be forever visible (if only to me.)

I mention money first so as to prepare you for one harsh fact of life in TV-Land: while TV does have it all, it hardly ever has all of it at once. But cheer up, because this isn't life; it's learning.

For You, Money Is no Object

Grand Tour Parisian Onion Soup doesn't actually exist. Your commercial will never be produced, so it's not going to cost you or anyone else a penny to give it everything you want. You're free to do anything. If you want two hundred beautiful dancers in long sequined gowns with ostrich feather headdresses eating onion soup as they dance up and down the steps of the Eiffel Tower under a starry sky, put them there.

Whatever you decide to do, just be sure you have a convincing reason for your choice and a real conviction that it's the best way to sell onion soup. Now let's quit the fantasy and get to work.

The Storyboard

The storyboard is to TV what a rough layout is to print. That means it's only a *statement of intentions*, a way to communicate an idea.

The storyboard can't be taken literally, because it can't actually do anything that TV can—it can't move, it can't sing, and because it shows a sequence of motionless frames, it can't look like a continuous performance.

What a Storyboard Can Show

A storyboard can show:

- what kinds of scenes you want to shoot.
- how many scenes there will be.
- in what sequence the scenes will be viewed.
- how many actors there will be.
- what the actors will look like, more or less.
- what action takes place in each scene.
- how long each scene takes.
- what words are said on-screen by actors.
- what words are said off-screen by a voice-over.
- what SFX are required in each scene.
- what kind of music will be heard.
- what optical effects will be used and where.
- what supers (printed words superimposed on the picture) will be used.

That's a lot of information. But, because of the many ways in which a storyboard is used, all of that information must be included.

A Storyboard Helps Sell the Idea

A storyboard helps you explain to your creative director and account manager exactly what you want to do. Once it is approved by them, you'll use the storyboard to explain the idea to your client. This is never easy, because clients seldom have the ability to visualize. For this reason, your board should be clear and convincing about visuals and their relationship to words, SFX, and music. If your client approves the commercial, the next use of the storyboard is even trickier, because you'll have no control over how it's presented.

Legal Clearance

After it is approved by the creative director, account manager, and client, the storyboard has to go to the client company's legal department and the lawyers at the NAB (National Association of Broadcasters) for clearance.

These lawyers may challenge a claim, such as "the only soup," and demand documentation. They may challenge a visual, such as "Is this man a real chef or a model?" They may ask for a legal disclaimer to be on screen if the man is a model. I know this sounds silly, but it often happens. You're free to challenge them, and sometimes they do change their minds, but don't bet on it.

When you've got the client's lawyers and the networks' clearance departments to sign off on a commercial, the storyboard comes into play again.

The Storyboard Drives the Production Specs

The storyboard acts as a set of specifications to help production companies understand what it will take to produce the spot. This enables them to come up with a price for the production.

The production company estimates the number of days of shooting time their director requires, which scenes can be shot on location, and which will best be shot on a stage set. Then, they figure out how much film or tape will be needed and what the film costs will be. If you use film, laboratory costs will be calculated as well. The production company also includes the cost of editing in their bids, unless your producer tells them you want to work with an independent editor. They work out the cost of equipment they will need or rent, how many extras the director wants in addition to the actors you've called for, what the sets, props and wardrobe will cost, what they will have to pay for the use of a location and for municipal permits and off-duty traffic cops, and how much electricity will be used for lighting. They work out how many people are needed for the crew and what the payroll will be, and they estimate the cost of breakfast and lunch on the set for the crew and production company, the agency people, and the client people. Bids often even include the cost of a "wrap dinner" for the agency and client. (When a shoot is completed, it's called "a wrap.")

Because of the complexity of this bidding process, your storyboard should be as complete a guide to the production as possible, without getting bogged down in details that would only confuse your client. Don't panic. A complex bid doesn't require a complex storyboard. In fact, it can be as simple as a single picture.

The Key Frame Storyboard

This kind of storyboard shows only one picture. It's the one scene that is the key to the entire visual.

For example, suppose you decided, back when we started thinking about print for Grand Tour Soups, that you liked that picture of the French family in their dining room with a view of the Eiffel Tower framed in the window. Suppose that's what you want to film, in a documentary style, with the actors speaking French and with many cuts to different family members eating and enjoying onion soup, plus shots of soup on the stove, soup being ladled into bowls, etc.

In this example you could use the full shot of the whole family at table, with the Eiffel Tower in the background, as the *key visual*. Your storyboard layout would look like this:

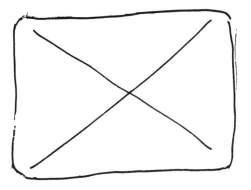

VIDEO

VO

SFX & MUSIC

How to Make Your Key Frame

This particular key frame is a tough picture to draw, because there are too many people and too much is going on. Look in magazines and stock photo books for a picture of a large family at a table and trace it. The people don't have to look French. After you've traced them nobody will know what they look like.

In the space labeled VIDEO, write a description of the action. Clarify if you want to show a close-up (write it as CU) of a person eating or a medium close-up (MCU) of two people and an extreme close-up (ECU) of soup. You'll also want a final shot of a can of Grand Tour Parisian Onion Soup, probably with a *super* (words superimposed on the picture).

In the space labeled V.O. (for voice-over), start by describing the announcer. Tell us if the announcer is a man or woman and whether he or she is speaking in an American accent or in a French one. Then, put in the copy.

In the space labeled SFX & MUSIC, say that we will hear the family speaking French, plus the natural sounds of serving and dining, such as spoons clinking on china. If you want a music bed for atmosphere, be sure to say so.

That's how to make a storyboard come alive with just one frame and some good writing. It could be a pretty commercial. But there's another, more usual way to show it in a storyboard.

How to Think Your Way Through a Storyboard

Before you start to write or draw, develop a plan. Here's an example of how to plan the "French Family" spot.

1. Establish the scene.

2. Move to the kitchen to let the viewer know that this is about soup.

3. Return to the family.

4. Return to the kitchen to build appetite and anticipation and show a serving suggestion.

5. See the family enjoying the soup.

6. See American consumers enjoying the soup at home.

7. Show the can.

This is a simple, logical construction, and it is the easiest and best way for you to visualize a commercial. Before you start to work out the number of frames you'll need, the copy, and the audio directions, make sure you work up a list like that one. The purpose of the list is not merely to show the order of scenes but to be sure the ad covers everything you want to show. After you've made your list, then you can reexamine it and think your way though the spot.

It is possible to make many structures from the above list of scenes. For instance, you could start the spot in an American home, with a couple eating soup and the man saying, "We haven't had onion soup this good since. . ." And then you could dissolve to the French dining room as the American wife says (V.O.) ". . . since Mama Dupont made it for us."

Assignment

How many other ways can you think of to use these scenes? Could you start with the kitchen scenes? Could you start with the family eating soup? Could you start with the can of Grand Tour Parisian Onion Soup?

If you were to start with the can, where would you go from there? And how would you make an interesting and memorable transition?

Try to visualize how a special effect could help you. Suppose the announcer's starting copy is "When you open a can of Grand Tour Parisian Onion Soup, it's like a magic trip to Paris."

Think about it. Try a few different structures. If you like one, write a script and make a rough working storyboard.

The Working Storyboard

The working storyboard is the most commonly used format. It will take approximately sixteen frames to show the French Family commercial (the standard storyboard pad has eight frames per page). The storyboard pad will look something like this:

The boxes with the rounded corners, reminiscent of TV screens, are where the drawings will appear. The squared boxes below will contain copy, video directions, and indications of SFX and music.

You will probably want to open with the whole family at table, as this is an establishing scene and one you will want to return to more than once. In production, this shot is called a *master*. You will want other frames as well, some showing one or two of these people in CU or MCU and some showing ECUs of steaming soup.

While it may appear in the final cut that your commercial is taking place in one location, it may actually have three *sets* and many *scenes*. One set is the dining room. Another is in the kitchen, where soup is being ladled from a pot on the stove into bowls, toast croutons are floated on the soup, and cheese is sprinkled over it. The third set may be only a tabletop, or it may be a limbo background, where you will shoot the can of soup.

A scene is any shot that requires a change of lighting and camera position. In shooting, the scene numbers may have little or nothing to do with the order in which these scenes appear in the finished commercial. These numbers only designate the order in which they are shot.

The director will shoot all of the dining room scenes in sequence. Then, he can strike the set (dismantle it or, if shooting on location, remove the props, the lights, and the camera) and go to the next set, which is the kitchen. On the storyboard, each of the scenes may be represented by one or more frames, depending on the action that takes place, the amount of copy to be read, or both. Sometimes the voice-over will have very few words to say, even though they will be said while several scenes are shown.

Moving Between Scenes

To go from one scene to another, you can:

- **Cut**, which means an abrupt end to one scene and an equally abrupt start of the next. Take care to insure that your cuts are logical, so that the viewers know where they are when you take them from one place to another.

- **Dissolve** (write it as DISS), which involves overlapping of the end of one scene that is fading out with the start of another that is fading in. In film, dissolve is an optical effect done in the lab. If you shoot with videotape instead of film, dissolves are done electronically during editing. There are slow dissolves, which tend to be dreamy. Normal dissolves are conventional film shorthand, understood by all viewers to indicate a change of time or place. Some dissolves are so short that they are called "soft cuts."

Let's say your edited commercial scene sequences will be like this:

- Open on the French family waiting for soup.

- Cut to soup being ladled.

- Cut to some family members laughing and pouring wine.

- Cut to ladling soup from the pot.

- Dissolve to toast and cheese being put in the soup bowls.

- Cut to family, still with no soup.

- Cut to the oven scene.

- Dissolve to bowl of soup being placed on table.

- Cut to sequence of four quick-cut frames showing family members eating and enjoying.

- Dissolve to pouring Grand Tour Soup from can to a different pot on a different stove.

- Dissolve to woman in American kitchen taking soup bowls from oven.

- Cut to American couple at table enjoying soup.

- Cut to beauty shot of Grant Tour Soup Can.

(For some inexplicable reason, a shot of the product is called a "beauty shot.")

Writing the Copy

Now that we've mapped out the scenes, let's start to build the copy for the announcer. The announcer might open the spot by saying something like this: "In Paris, onion soup is not just soup. Properly made, it's a cause for passion." That's just six seconds of copy, but you may want it to run over your first four scenes, which might last for nine seconds. You indicate it like this:

V.O.: "In Paris. . .
VIDEO: FRENCH FAMILY AT TABLE
WAITING FOR FOOD, POURING WINE,
EATING BREAD

SFX: FAMILY SPEAKING FRENCH
NATURAL SOUNDS
MUSIC: FRENCH ACCORDION BED

V.O.: "...onion soup is not just soup."

VIDEO: MCU SOUP LADLED INTO BOWLS

SFX: VOICES, FRENCH MUSIC UP

Note that "Up" means more volume. But when you want less volume, don't write "Down." In filmspeak, you write "Under." Filmspeak isn't always logical, but then, neither is regular speech. After all, you lace up your shoes, but you don't lace them down.

Notice that frame 3 has no voice-over. This wordless scene allows us to take a moment to get to know the family and to absorb some French ambiance while we build some anticipation for that soup.

V.O.: "Properly made, it's a cause for passion."

VIDEO: CU PUTTING TOAST ON SOUP
AND SPRINKLING CHEESE ON IT.

SFX: FAMILY TALK AND TABLE SOUNDS
UNDER, MUSIC BED STEADY.

You now have a little over twenty seconds remaining to complete the rest of your message. My own preference is not to say in words what you can show in pictures. For example, because I've given a clear, understandable serving suggestion in the video, there's no need to say, "Just float toast on the soup, put cheese on top, and heat under the broiler for a few seconds until the cheese melts." That would be a waste of seven precious seconds.

Now, the following assignment gives you the chance to complete this 16-frame working storyboard.

Assignment

Complete the preceding working storyboard.

Start by writing it as a script. The script form is simple. Use two columns. The left-hand column, headed VIDEO, tells what you want to be shown. It also is used to indicate the SFX and music. The right-hand column is reserved for spoken words.

Write the announcer's copy and the video and audio instructions. Place them so that they are aligned on the paper with the announcer's copy at the point where they will occur.

Here's the script for what I've written so far, just to be sure that you understand the form.

GRAND TOUR SOUPS
TV :30
"FRENCH FAMILY"

VIDEO	AUDIO
FRENCH FAMILY AT TABLE, WAITING FOR FOOD. EIFFEL TOWER SEEN THROUGH A WINDOW BEHIND. SFX: FAMILY SPEAKING FRENCH, PLUS NATURAL SOUND. MUSIC: FRENCH ACCORDION BED THROUGHOUT.	(MALE AMERICAN ANNOUNCER V.O.) In Paris...
CUT TO MCU ONION SOUP BEING LADLED INTO BOWLS AT KITCHEN STOVE.	...onion soup is not just soup.
CUT TO FAMILY AT TABLE. FRENCH CONVERSATION, ALL TAKING AT ONCE. SFX AND MUSIC UP.	
CUT TO CU HAND FLOATING TOAST AND CHEESE ON SOUP.	Properly made, it's a cause for celebration.

Please remember, those words are mine, not yours. If you want to write something else, go ahead, but do complete this particular spot. When you're done, I want you to use your rough drawing skills to make the storyboard.

You can use a storyboard pad, available in most art supply stores. If they have black cardboard frames with cutouts for each picture area and word area, buy some of these (they're called masks) and forget the storyboard pads. Masks make assembling a storyboard easy, because you don't have to draw on the storyboard pad. You can draw on any paper you like after tracing the outline of a storyboard mask. Then, hold your drawing in place with tape that the mask will hide.

You can also type your copy and video and audio instructions and tape them in the boxes. Or, you could type it on pressure-sensitive, gummed labels. Practice making working storyboards like this for whatever assignments you want to give yourself. You'll be using this form for most of your real world TV work.

The Shooting Board

You're not likely to ever make a shooting board, but it's a good idea to know what one is. The shooting board is a 30-frame board, one frame for each second, that is used by some directors for precise planning. The frames are thumbnails and seldom include copy, video direction, SFX, or anything but action.

The purpose of a shooting board is to establish what will be shot and how much time will be needed for each take. (A take is the time the camera is running on a scene, from the moment the director says "action" to the moment he or she says "cut.") In practice, the take will include more film or tape footage than you need, both before the action and after it. These bits are called "heads" and "tails," and they give the film editor flexibility in assembling and timing the commercial. The shooting board indicates the timing of takes more precisely than a working board can, by showing a scene and extending it with an arrowed line through as many seconds as it will take.

What this shows is that, although the spoken words, "In France. . ." take only one second to say, the director plans to use two and a half seconds for this scene. He wants the viewers to have the time to absorb and understand the setting, and he wants to allow a little time before the announcer talks so that the viewers can hear the music and the SFX.

You may never get to see a shooting board, but if you do, it will most probably not show up until the preproduction meeting (we'll get to that later) and again on the set. But you now know what one is and what it's for.

An Exercise In TV Visualization

Remember the magazine ad we created with the French chef? I liked it because it was simple and hardworking and it sure had legs. Let's pretend now that I'm the client and that you have me firmly sold on that print campaign. I'm not in the least interested in looking at foreign families eating soup. I want you to develop a TV campaign that will fit with and support my print advertising.

Assignment

Create a TV spot that is the counterpart of the French Chef magazine ad.

Remember to think first, write and draw later. Here are some of the elements of your board that should be included if this ad is to go with the print:

- A French Chef saying something nice about the soup in French

- A translation of what the chef is saying

- This could be in spoken English or in a typographic super, a *mortise*, or a *title*. (A super is superimposed on a picture. A mortise is a frame with type in it that has been cut out of the picture. A title is just type on a flat background.)

- A close-up of soup, for appetite appeal

- A picture of the Grand Tour can

On the face of it, this list doesn't look like a very interesting or engaging commercial. But it isn't a commercial; it's only a list. This list tells what you have to do, but it doesn't tell you how to do it or offer other ideas. Now it's up to you to visualize what else you could do in order to:

1. get the viewers' attention and hold it.

2. make the viewers hungry for that soup.

3. convince the viewers that this is the most authentically delicious onion soup they can get outside of Paris.

4. make them remember the brand name and the way the can looks.

After you have visualized some ideas, make a key frame board. Then, make a working board.

Are We Having Fun Yet?

The best fun I know in advertising is actually producing, shooting, and completing a commercial. But, before most clients will let you do it, there's one more rite of passage you must endure.

Animatics

Animatics are commonly used to test commercials for clarity of communication, persuasion, and memorability. An animatic is really just an expanded working storyboard that has frames large enough to be videotaped. The visuals will be well drawn, in full color, by a professional illustrator. You will probably have the illustrator draw more frames than you used in the working board, so that, with the use of quick cuts and dissolves, you can give some impression of movement.

You can have some actual movement, too. For example, if you want to show the French Chef lifting a spoon to his mouth to taste, the arm and hand holding the spoon can be drawn and cemented to a clear acetate sheet. When the frame of the French Chef is put in place under the TV camera, the arm overlay can be put over it, in a position just below that seen by the camera. The overlay can then be rotated by hand, so that the spoon comes to the Chef's mouth. At that point, the picture can be dissolved into the next image: a picture of the chef, with the spoon at his mouth, now showing a surprised smile. This will almost look like motion.

Unfortunately, it won't look like life. Don't expect or ask too much from an animatic. For instance, you'll never be able to get a satisfactory approximation of someone speaking to you. You just can't do lip synchronization (write it as "lip-synch") with a drawing unless you do full animation, like in a Disney film, and full animation costs more to do than making film or tape with live actors.

Why Animatics?

Given that animatics are such awkward and limiting tools, why are they used for testing? The reason is money. Because the *average* price of producing a 30-second spot in 1990 was an estimated $157,500, and an animatic could be produced for as little as $5,000, you can see why animatics are used to test commercials before a commitment to shoot is made.

My one inflexible rule for making successful animatics is to first make a professional, "broadcast quality" sound track. This means getting good actors for your voices. Don't do a homemade track with coworkers playing the parts. It also means getting the music and SFX you will use in the finished commercial. If you need original music—for a jingle, for example—have it composed and produced.

How Music Communicates

I've mentioned music as an element several times, but it needs more than a mere mention. Music is a truly powerful communicator. I'll tell you how it can work for you.

Music is the foundation of many TV commercials, especially in such categories as soft drinks, fashion, travel destinations, and many more. These days, more often than not, the use of music involves buying commercial rights to a well-known song that kind of fits the mood a creative team wants to project while they show the lifestyle of the target audience. There's nothing wrong with that except that the music may wind up being the tail that wags the dog. The power of the music as a communication tool is left untapped.

How Music Can Change Meaning

Earlier I said that I would show you how music can intensify or even change the meaning of what you see on the screen. Start by visualizing this picture. Great, formal wrought-iron gates hung on massive stone pillars swing open to allow a perfect, gleaming Rolls Royce from about 1940 to pass through. The car goes by us to swing up a curving drive towards a mansion. We can't see the passengers. We hear a big orchestra playing "Rule Britannia." Who might be in the car? What year is it? What decade?

You get the point. And I'm sure you'll give careful thought about what kind of music you want when you write your next commercial.

Assignment

To test the effects of music on our Rolls-Royce scene, try these variations.

1. Rewind the film. Start the Rolls through the gates again. This time we hear the soundtrack from the Beatles' "A Hard Day's Night." Who might be in the car now? What year or decade is it now?
2. Rewind the film again. Cue the Rolls. Now play Madonna singing "Material Girl." Look how everything's changed.
3. Let's do it again, but this time the music has been composed for the film. It is heavy, ominous, even eerie. Sad sopranos and violins wail. What's going on here?
4. Want to try a pass with "Yankee Doodle Dandy"? There's a whole new story about to unfold.
5. And if you want to move the scene out of England, view the sequence again while playing "My Old Kentucky Home."

Don't just settle for what's popular at the moment or for what you personally like. Use what works to *communicate*.

The Music Makers

Most music houses will prepare a demo for your animatic pretty cheaply, often using synthesized music instead of live musicians. However, if the music has lyrics they will insist, as should you, on good, professional studio singers.

Your finished sound track, with music, SFX, and voices mixed at the right levels, will act as a guide for the animatic production. Its timing will cue the timings of the takes. You'll watch your tape editor build the spot, one scene after the other, in the order in which they are to appear. Soon you will have a finished animatic that is ready to be put to the test with consumers.

You're going to hate the animatic because of what it's unable to do. A partial list of what animatics can't do reads like a list of the most effective things a commercial can do. Animatics can't:

- Be believable presenters.

- Give a convincing product demonstration.

- Act, sing, and dance.

- Be humorous.

- Project a personality.

- Create a mood.

- Indicate special film effects.

- Generate appetite appeal.

Photomatics

Because of these limitations, some animatics, called *photomatics*, are made not with drawings but with still photographs. Because they are made the same way as animatics, photomatics suffer many of the same limitations, including lack of movement, acting, emotion, demonstration, etc. But for some categories, photomatics make much better sense and are worth the expense. Shampoos, hair conditioners, and hair coloring, for instance, depend on showing beautiful hair. You can do this with a photo far better than you can with a drawing or a painting. Food products have to look delicious enough for the viewer to want to eat off the screen. I can't imagine a drawing of a plate of spaghetti and meat sauce that could look worth eating, especially when compared to a good photo.

You can probably think of a dozen more products, services, and situations that would be better presented in a photo than in an illustration. Remember, however, that the photomatic is put together exactly the same as the animatic and you'll hate it only a little less than an animatic when it's finished.

In this chapter you learned what a storyboard is and how it's used to present to client, to clear with lawyers and broadcasters, and to start the bidding and production process. You now understand the different kinds of storyboards: key frame, working, and shooting. You started learning storyboard and production language and abbreviations, and you now have an idea what animatics and photomatics are. Most important, you've learned how to think your way through a storyboard.

New Key Terms

* animatic

* beauty shot

* CU

* cut

* dissolve

* ECU

* heads and tails

* master shot

* MCU

* mortise

* music bed

* photomatic

* scene

* set

* strike (a set)

* super

* take

* title

* wrap

CHAPTER 12

It's Show Time!

In this chapter you will

- meet your producer.
- evaluate directors' show reels.
- learn how to read production bids.
- understand the importance of the pre-pro meeting.
- find out about pre-casting, callbacks, and casting.
- meet all the specialists.
- review editing and all other post-production steps.

Congratulations! Your hated animatic or photomatic scored well in testing and your client has given you the okay to get on with actual production.

Now Comes the Hard Part

I'll never forget the first time I received the okay for production or what my creative director told me. "From here on," he said, "you're at the mercy of experts."

It's easy to lose control of a production and to have it fail to come out the way you visualized it and sold it to your client. For example, you may have written and sold a commercial whose appeal was a subtle use of sly wit and humor. The director, however, sees it as an opportunity for broad comedy. He can alter the whole tone of the spot and damage it badly without changing a word or a situation.

There are ways to prevent this sort of thing from ever happening. This section will give you enough knowledge of the production process to help prevent a wide range of disasters and to help you understand what's going on during your first experience with this special world.

The TV Production Track

Getting started depends very much on where you work and on what resources, both human and mechanical, you have available. If you're doing your first commercial, the odds are that you work at an ad agency. After all, what client is going to trust a neophyte, without an organization to back him or her up, to wisely spend tens of thousands to hundreds of thousands of the client's dollars?

The Producer

The first step is for the creative team to meet with an agency producer, who then becomes the third member of the creative team. You take the producer through the storyboard, explaining its look, its tone, and its attitude. From this meeting you'll arrive at a clear, common understanding of casting specifications, locations or sets, wardrobe, opticals and effects, music requirements, and all other elements of the final production.

The Director

Your producer should have some suggestions about which directors and production companies would be best for the job. Then, he or she arranges to have some directors' show reels delivered for the three of you to view the next day.

Viewing Show Reels

First, pause to remember that the director didn't write those spots; he or she simply tried to get the most from them. Look carefully and analytically even at commercials you hate. See whether the scenes were interestingly framed, how well the actors were directed for performance, how good the lighting looks, and note whether the camera moves were well-controlled.

Look at more than one or two of the directors' spots. Take the time to view the entire reel, so that you can identify the director's main strength.

Specialists

There are all kinds of directors. Some specialize in *performance*, which means getting the most out of actors. Some specialize in *action*, where performance is not necessary or is at most secondary. These are the kinds of spots that feature scenes such as athletic events, Spring Break beach parties, cattle roundups, car chases, and the like. Some directors specialize in *comedy*. Some directors specialize in *period pieces*, such as a general store of the 1800s, authentically propped and wardrobed and lit as if by gaslight. Some specialize in food and, like their still-photo counterparts, are called *tabletop* directors.

But specializing in one of these areas only means it's a major strength. It doesn't mean a director can't do other things well, too. When you review the show reels with your producer, look for capabilities, for assurance that the director can do what you want. Don't look literally to see if he or she has already done a spot or two that's just like yours. There has never been a spot that's just like yours.

When you've viewed a show reel, make a few notes about the director and whether you think he or she is a possible option for this production. Even if you think not but are impressed by some other ability that you may want to use on another spot some day, make notes and keep them. Get to know about directors. At the very least, you and your partners should identify three directors to whom you would trust your production.

Getting Bids and Reviewing Them

The process of securing and reviewing bids is your producer's job. First, the producer gets typing-paper-sized storyboards made up. He or she then calls in producers from the three production companies to explain the boards and give any specs not indicated on them.

This presentation is either done one production company at a time or in an open bid meeting. I happen to prefer the open bid meeting, because it's a certainty that the producers from all the production companies will hear the same things. Also, each of the producers can benefit from questions asked by any of the others. A final benefit of the open bid meeting is that it doesn't put the entire burden of communication on your producer. The meeting can be attended by all members of the creative team and, if useful, the account management team. You'll never get all of those individuals together for three separate bid meetings.

Buyer Beware!

Bids are usually received in four or five days. The bid sheets are very complex, covering all the costs of the production one line at a time, so you should learn how to review them. Don't just look at the bottom line (as your client will want to do) to see which is the cheapest. Look further, to see what you're *not* getting from the lowest-cost company and to see what *added value* you may be getting from the top or middle bidder.

You may find that the low bid calls for one 12-hour day of shooting, while the highest bid has been based on a 10-hour day and an 8-hour day. You may find that the low bidder has estimated using 30 percent less film stock than the high bidder. It's pretty obvious that the more time a director has, the more attention he can pay to detail. He can perfect his lighting, take an hour for that one extra set-up, and work patiently with the actors to get the very best performance from them. It's also obvious that the more film is shot, the more options you and your editor will have. So the high bidder—or the middle one—may be a better choice than the low bidder.

What it all comes down to is whether, in your judgment, the added cost will pay off in significant added value. There's also the question of whether your client's budget can stand the price of the best. Your account manager should have given your producer some notion of what the client is prepared to pay before the show reels were requested and reviewed. In short, if all you can afford is a Hyundai, stay out of BMW showrooms.

The Preproduction Meeting

The first step after hiring a production company is the preproduction meeting, called a *pre-pro*. The purpose of the pre-pro is to assure that everyone who will be involved in the production will share a common understanding of the commercial, including its look, its tone, and its intentions.

Who Attends the Pre-Pro?

The pre-pro is a critical meeting and should be attended by everyone who will have a say in the production. Someone from the client must be there. If there are several client people who will be involved in the production in any way, even if only as observers on the set, try to get them to attend.

On the agency side, your account manager must attend and your creative director should also be present. Of course, the creative team will be in attendance.

On the production company side, attendees should include the director, a producer, perhaps a unit manager, someone in charge of casting, a set designer if the director has opted for sets, and a location scout if locations are to be used. If wardrobe is to be in any way special, a wardrobe person may also be present.

There may be other people in attendance as well, and some of their job titles will tell you little. As the meeting progresses, it will become increasingly clear what responsibilities each person has.

How the meeting is run   The pre-pro is usually run by the director. Using your working storyboard as a reference, the director tells the group his or her vision of the commercial. This is the right time to be sure that everyone is marching to the same drummer. If there are differences of opinion, now's the time to air them.

For example, the director might be visualizing soft-focus images with pastel shades, filmed in a sort of hazy, romantic lighting. The creative team members, however, are thinking in terms of sharp, documentary images with subdued color and strong shadows. Reach an agreement now, because it will be too late when you get on the set and see the director's hazy lighting and fog machine for the first time.

The meeting gets more specific from this point forward, usually moving on to casting.

Casting   In many cases the director will have done some pre-casting. With this, actors (who are referred to as *talent*, whether they have any or not) have already been called in to read a line or two to a video camera. At this point, the group reviews the casting tapes. You might actually find some of the talent you need on these tapes, but it's not usual. This first review is really a way of getting more refined casting specs. You may, for one example, feel that the talent called in were the wrong ages. That will tell the casting director what to do next. You may find one or two possibles on the first review. Say, for example, that there's a talent who has exactly the look you want, but you don't like the way he delivered the line. In this case, the actor will be put on callback, which means he will come in again, and the director and you will work with him to see if he can give a better reading. Callbacks happen a day or two after the pre-pro, but the decision on whether to have any is made at the pre-pro.

If none of the talent is close enough to what you want, the casting director continues the search for talent. You will review new tapes in a day or two, or if you want, you can attend the casting session.

Sets and Locations

If sets are to be used, the set designer shows some preliminary sketches for discussion. If shooting is to take place on location, the location scout passes around an album of Polaroids. Several possible locations are then identified. Those locations will be visited by you and the director in the next day or two for final approval.

One by one, all elements of the shoot are discussed and agreed upon—wardrobe, special props, special makeup, how the product will be shot, and what if any role music will play. A thorough pre-pro for an average production will take three to four hours.

Production

A week or so after the pre-pro, actual production starts. The Big Day has come. The crew has been called for 6:00 A.M., you were told to show up around 7:00 A.M., and the client was told to come at 8:30 A.M. or so. You arrive early and find a well-populated chaos.

Who Are all Those People?

The people on the set are: the director, the cameraman or operator, the lighting director, the assistant director, the assistant cameraman, sound, continuity, grips, the key grip, electricians, gaffers, set constructors, props, the home economist, wardrobe, makeup, the unit manager, the producer, a still photographer, and a production assistant. The responsibilities of these individuals are outlined in the appendix at the end of this chapter.

Your Job: Focus on Everything

Given the normal crew, you've now got twenty-eight to thirty production company people on the set, plus talent, plus four from the agency, plus at least one from your client. It's pretty crowded. Now you understand what I meant by being at the mercy of experts. Each of the major people in this production *is* an expert, and there is a great temptation for you to stand aside, shut up, ask no questions, and make no suggestions. Don't do it.

Get your energy up. Focus your full attention on *everything* that's happening. If you have a question, ask it. If you have a suggestion, make it. Don't worry about looking dumb. You'll look a lot dumber if you have no answer when your creative director reviews the footage with you and says, "Why did you shoot it *that* way?" Remember, even your very first shoot is yours. It will always mean more to you than to anyone else. Don't let it get away from you.

The Postproduction Track

If you shoot with tape, there is no next-day review of the takes with the director, because you will have already seen and timed them all during the shoot.

If you work with film, there's often a videotape hookup that lets you see the action as the camera sees it and allows playback so that you can judge performance and timing before going on to the next scene. The quality of this video monitor is pretty bad black and white, however, so you can't judge lighting and color from it.

Dailies

Because of the poor quality of the videotape monitor, you will want to review the *dailies* with the director. The dailies are overnight prints, also not of the best quality, but they are good enough for your team and the director to decide whether you've got what you need.

If you don't have what you need, the production company will be prepared to reshoot what they have to, at their expense. This can be a financial disaster for them and it almost never happens.

Editing

Assuming that everything is acceptable, the next step is editing, which means cutting the film and assembling it to make a coherent story. Many directors request the right to "first cut," and some even get it written into their contracts. If the director wants the first cut, just say yes. There's no rule that you have to use it. When you've looked it over, say that it's great and then meet with your editor, who will become the final member of your creative team.

It is an axiom in the film business that "movies aren't made; they're re-made." This doesn't mean reshooting. It means that the way an editor arranges the scene is an art form that can make an enormous difference in the final film.

The editor might suggest a variety of effects you haven't considered, such as slow motion for a portion of the film, showing some scenes in black and white, or blowing up some CU scenes to make them ECU. The editor may suggest starting the story at a different point than the one shown in the storyboard or, possibly, adding some SFX you didn't think about.

As you review the takes, you and your team will tell the editor which ones you like. He or she will make notes of scene and take numbers and may add some personal choices to yours. All of these choices are called *selects*.

If you started with film, it will probably be transferred to tape for electronic editing at this point.

The editing machines Some editors still prefer the old method of editing with a *work print*. In this process they physically cut the film and put it together with transparent tape, viewing it on an editing machine as they go.

The old standard editing machine is the Moviola. It's a noisy, clattering piece of almost Victorian-looking machinery that restricts viewing to a tiny screen, about four by five inches in size. For reasons I've never understood, the Moviola is still preferred by many of the best editors. The flat-bed editing machine is a great improvement. This machine runs quietly, and its TV-sized screen can be viewed by three or four people at the same time. Puzzlingly, most editors don't like them.

In my opinion, nothing works as well as tape. In tape editing, you can find a scene almost instantly (via computer filing), view it, make the cut or dissolve to the next scene, and look at a preview to see how it works. You can build an entire spot, store it, and try again, starting from a whole different place. Unlike film editing, you don't have to take your work print apart and reassemble it. And when you're done with version #2 you can view both versions and see which you like best. In fact, you can make as many versions of the spot as you want, until you've got what you like.

If your shoot began with film, the videotape transfer for editing will carry frame numbers, which will allow the film lab to identify the finally selected takes and assemble them in the negative just as you wanted.

After Editing

After editing, the spot you have created is called a rough cut. The rough cut must be shown to the creative director, and then to your client, for approval.

Before you show it, explain what, if anything, is missing from the film. Typically, a rough cut will be unfinished in some of the following ways:

- The music will probably be the demo track and not the finished performance.

- SFX will need to be added.

- Opticals, including supers and titles, will be indicated with crayon marks or by a blank piece of black or white tape, called a *slug*.

- The V.O. announcer will probably be a *scratch track*, a rough recording that is often made by the talent in the agency's studio as a casting tape. The scratch track is used for guidance in editing. The final reading will have to be recorded.

Be sure you explain all these missing elements *before* showing the rough cut to anyone. Otherwise, it will sound like you're making excuses rather than clarifying your presentation.

Finishing Touches

After the client approves the rough cut, your next job will be to complete all of the final touches that remain. The announcer and the final music need to be recorded, and your editor will get additional needed SFX. Then, with the help of your editor, all of these elements will be put together in a *mix*. In a specialized mix studio, your editor *lines up*, or synchronizes, the picture, voice track, music track, and SFX track. Together, you decide on the best balance of the sound levels of the tracks.

Don't worry about getting all of this straight. In the real world of ad agencies, you'll get on-the-job training. Before you get to shoot your first spot, you'll go with experienced creative teams to see a few shots, sit in on a pre-pro or two, attend an editing session and a mix. By the time it's your turn, you'll be ready for it.

The Final Product: Videotape

The production is now almost complete. All that remains is a transfer to videotape. Even if you shoot on film, the final spots will go to the TV stations in the form of videocassettes. This is done because film is easily scratched and could be damaged by the technicians at TV stations. You're safer with tape.

In this chapter you've learned what an agency producer does, from suggesting directors and viewing their show reels with you to specifying and evaluating bids. You've seen how a pre-pro can effect your production, met the director and other key specialists, and developed an understanding of the complexity of a shoot and the postproduction process.

* callbacks

* dailies

* flat-bed editing machine

* line up (tracks)

* mix

* Moviola editing machine

* rough cut

* selects

* scratch track

* show reel

* talent

* work print

CHAPTER 12

Who are all of those people, and what are they doing on the set?

The **director** is in charge of the chaos, out of which she will bring order. Everyone on the set answers to the director.

The **cameraman**, or operator, runs the camera. He frames the shot, rehearses the camera moves, and keeps a careful eye on the scene to see, for example, if any of the lighting creates a flare as the camera pans by. (A *pan* is a lateral move, where the camera is swiveled from one side to the other on the tripod.)

The **lighting director** is in charge of creating the lighting called for by the director. Some directors serve as their own lighting directors.

The **assistant director** does not direct; she assists the director. Her main job is marking scene and take numbers on the *slate*, which she holds in front of the camera to be shot for a few seconds before a new take is made. If the production is in synch sound, the slate will have a *clapper*, painted with opposing stripes, hinged on top of it.

The assistant director will "slate the take" by calling the scene and take numbers aloud and then slapping the clapper arm down. Later, the editor will use these visible and audible cues to synchronize the sound and the picture. (By the way, the slate is not made of slate. It was once, but now it's a board. The scene and take numbers are taped on it.)

The **assistant camerman** loads the film in the camera, keeps track of how much film is left in the magazine (called the *mag*), and tells the cameraman when it's time to reload. He also changes lenses as required and marks positions for zooms. The assistant operates the zoom lens because he's in a position to see the start and stop cue marks he taped on the lens. (The operator makes the pans himself, because only he can see how they look while they're happening.) The assistant cameraman is also responsible for reading the light meter, keeping the lenses clean, and many other mechanical functions.

Sound runs the recording equipment, cues the director for the next take by saying "speed" (which means his tape is running), and listens for stray sounds that shouldn't be there. Sound might be aware, through his earphones, of the hum of a motor that nobody else could hear but that will be picked up by the sensitive microphones. Sound is the only person on the set, other than the director, who is allowed to say "cut," meaning "stop making the take."

Continuity keeps track of the timings of takes and marks those that the director says should be printed. Continuity also makes sure that the commercial has enough footage to be edited for correct time.

Continuity's main job is to ensure that there are no mistakes in how the visuals will track. For example, if a character exits to the right in a scene, a return to the scene from the left would look wrong. The exit and the reentry may be filmed hours apart. Continuity reminds the director of the right-side exit when she sets up for the reentry. Continuity also makes sure that wardrobe is consistent. If one of the talent is wearing a blue shirt in a scene, he can't come back in the same scene in a white one, even though there was a reason to change to white for another scene that was shot in the intervening time. You will generally find Continuity seated very close to the camera, often under it, working intently with a stopwatch and taking copious notes on a clipboard full of forms.

Grips are the people who move things about and set up special rigs to hold reflectors, lights, and a host of other things. They are all-purpose craftsmen and can work miracles with a small assortment of specialized equipment. Some of their tools are:

- *Grip stands*, which are contraptions of pipes and clamps set on tripods. One of the clamps might hold a *flag*, which is a simple piece of cardboard set up to diminish the effect of a light. Another clamp might hold a prop that is to be seen in the foreground, such as a leafy branch.

- *Sandbags*, which are used to steady the grip stands.

- *Apples*, which are not fruit but sturdy boxes with a cut-out hand hold at each end. Early film makers used apple boxes to act as pedestals when something had to be set up a little higher. Today's apples come in different thicknesses: full apple, half apple, etc. the full apples get a lot of use on the set as stools, writing desks, and coffee tables.

The **key grip** is the boss of the grips. Her importance to a production can be judged by the fact that in feature films, the key grip often gets a credit.

Electricians hook up the maze of heavy cables, junction boxes, and power outlets that are needed to operate the camera and lights. On some locations electricians will set up a generator and make sure that it is hooded, muffled, and well away from sensitive microphones.

Gaffers are lighting technicians who set up and operate the lights. Their name comes from the days when all studio lighting was hung from the ceiling and could be moved and adjusted only with the use of long poles, called gaffs. The gaffer's job includes adjusting the direction the lights will aim and the intensity and color of the light. Stage lights can be modified by widening or narrowing small "barn doors," metal flaps on both sides of the lens. Light can be made less intense by inserting *silks* in the rings in front of the light; it can be colored by inserting transparent *gels* in the rings. Gaffers make these adjustments only when the director or lighting director tells them to.

Set constructors assemble the sets, which will actually have been built elsewhere. Their work will often include final painting, wallpapering, and anything else that could not be prefinished. When the director is finished shooting the set, the set constructors strike it.

Props is in charge of all the objects (called "properties") that will be seen in the production. Props will usually bring an assortment from which to choose, as there is almost never time to get down to such fine detail before shoot day. If a soup kettle is needed, there will be five or six varying sizes, kinds, and ages. There will be choices of bowls, all authentically traditional for Parisian Onion Soup. There will be a collection of ladles, tablecloths, bread baskets, tableware, wine glasses, etc.

The **home economist** will supervise the final preparation of the soup, adding the correct kind of toasted French bread rounds and the proper kind and amount of cheese. If there are other foods that will be seen, the home economist will bring them or make them in the studio kitchen.

Wardrobe will bring a selection of clothes for each of the talent. The director may not make a final selection until she sees talent together in the setting. Then, composing the picture, the director will ask for choices of colors and styles.

Makeup's job usually includes hair, but not always. You will sometimes find both a makeup artist and a hair stylist on the same set.

The **unit manager** makes sure that everyone understands what's wanted and that everything is getting done. If an unanticipated piece of equipment is called for by the director, the unit manager makes the necessary phone call to locate it.

The **producer** (not yours, but the production company's) makes sure that nothing happens that will affect the cost of the production. If the director has a new idea not in the storyboard and not agreed to in the pre-pro, and you and your client decide that you'd like to shoot it, the producer will decide if the budget is large enough to handle it. If the modification is going to involve extra equipment, overtime, or more film, the producer will tell your producer how much extra expense will be involved. Your client can then either authorize or reject the change.

A **still photographer** is present on many sets in order to document the shoot.

A **production assistant** is an apprentice and "gopher" who is available to take care of anything that anyone might need.

Part Five

The Great Outdoors

CHAPTER 13

The Last Frontier

In this chapter you will

- see how good outdoor depends on a clear campaign concept.
- understand how outdoor challenges your concept.
- learn the simple rules and evaluate a campaign that ignores them.
- consider other forms of posters.

There's one more important exercise left in visual thinking—outdoor advertising, or billboards.

Facing the Challenge

I saved outdoor for last partly because it's the toughest medium to deal with. More important, because a billboard is the irreducible essence of a campaign, you usually don't do outdoor advertising until you've first developed a complete campaign.

What makes outdoor so difficult is the fact that your audience has its attention focused on driving a car, not on reading advertising. Also, that car is whizzing past the advertising at 60 miles per hour. If you actually get the driver's attention, you will only have it for about two seconds or less. To deliver an effective message in print in so short a time is a real challenge.

If you can create a good outdoor board for any campaign in your portfolio, it will be your assurance that the campaign really works, because it will show that you have a strong, clear, central selling idea. Are there any rules to follow when creating these ads? As always, yes and no.

The "Rules"

The Outdoor Advertising Institute says to make your billboard message largely visual and to use the fewest possible words. I think they suggest an absolute maximum of nine words. They're probably right about having a strong visual, but I think the word count is an arbitrary number. (I'm also sure they have some research to bear them out.) I think the keys are *simplicity* and *singularity*, however you achieve them, even if your concept breaks all the rules.

A Sample Rule Breaker

Helmut Krone and I once did a highly effective and award-winning outdoor campaign for Avis Rent-A-Car that deliberately broke all the rules. The boards carried no visuals, only black type on a white background. A typical board read, "Avis won't rent you a dirty Plymouth. No ifs, ands, or butts." Twelve words. No pictures.

What made this campaign work was the fact that nothing else on the roads to the airports looked even remotely like those billboards. Their starkness lured the eye. Also, because the target audience was frequent business fliers, our boards were only on major airport approach routes and our targets passed the billboards often. If they didn't get the whole message the first time, they would have other chances.

I don't mean to suggest that you try this technique. I'm only suggesting that all rules are meant to be challenged.

The Grand Tour Outdoors

Now let's think about what kind of outdoor to do for Grand Tour Soups. If you've been developing your own campaign, one I don't know about, you're on you own. But if you've been tracking with me, we can do a billboard together. Let's first think about it visually and conceptually, as usual.

Does the Idea Hold Up?

My first thought is that the "French Family" concept that was starting to look pretty attractive when we did it in TV doesn't look so good now. How can we make outdoor from it? Its images are too complex, too moody, and too dependent on casting, scenery, and props to make a big, clear singular image in the bright sunlight.

And now that we think of it, what was the central selling idea of that campaign?

Are you feeling, as I am, the emptiness at the core of that idea? I think, in fact, that it had no more real substance than the Eiffel Tower rocket ship with its crew of dancers. Confronted with the demands of outdoor, both of these ideas now appear to be entirely executional and not at all conceptual.

I never wrote the balance of the copy for that Parisian family TV commercial, because I didn't like the idea. But I did ask you to write it. Did you do it? If so, did you create a selling proposition and encapsulate it in a copy line strong enough to stand on its own on a billboard? If you did, congratulations. Now see if you can develop a simple visual that will work with your headline.

If, on the other hand, you stayed with my idea of the French chef tasting soup, all of your outdoor problems are solved. We've already done one billboard. It's just the magazine ad without the body copy and the picture of the bowl of soup. In fact, we've actually created more than a billboard; we've created a whole outdoor campaign. Just go from soup to soup, from chef to chef, and, with the right photos and fresh, surprising casting, you'll be able to keep the campaign alive and effective for a long time to come.

> *Main picture:* surprised and delighted chef (French, Chinese, German, etc.) tasting soup
> *Headline:* "Only in America!"
> *Signature:* Grand Tour Parisian Onion Soup
> *Minor picture:* can of soup, used almost as a logo

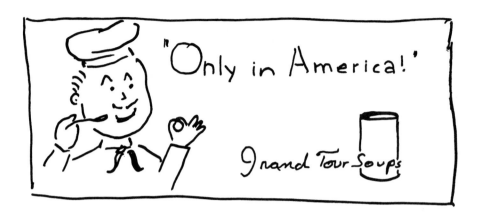

Simplify and Echo

Notice that I didn't put the Chef's headline words in a foreign language and then translate them. There just isn't time enough for a driver to read all that. I'm counting on the magazine ads, the radio, and the TV to do the job with foreign phrases. (I'm sure you remember that outdoor ads were to be phased in after the campaign launch.) I'm guessing that anyone who is familiar with the campaign will make the connection to the outdoor boards.

Not counting local billboards such as those that tell you the next McDonald's is four miles down the road, outdoor works best as a reminder of other advertising. For example, that Avis board of mine would never have worked if it hadn't echoed a well-established national campaign.

The Billboard Test

I strongly suggest that you test every campaign you create for your portfolio by trying to make it into a billboard. Even if you wrote a campaign of ads with long copy, full of information, if you can't make a billboard that encapsulates the theme of the campaign, then there is probably something wrong.

For an example of this, consider a campaign that's done almost everything right: BMW. Everything BMW does answers to a central selling theme: "The ultimate driving machine." You'd have no trouble writing informative, long copy ads for BMW based on the theme. At the same time, you'd have no trouble doing the billboard that just showed a picture of a BMW convertible with it's top down and the headline: "The ultimate tanning machine."

┌───┐

Assignment

- If you developed a campaign different from mine, create an outdoor board for Grand Tour Soups.
- Create an outdoor board for any current advertising campaign you like.
- Create a billboard for the Outdoor Advertising Institute. Its message is that outdoor advertising is an effective medium.

└───┘

Other Billboards and Posters

There are a few more simple facts you should know about outdoor. Outdoor includes more than big highway billboards.

The same thinking you use for these billboards also applies to those little posters you find mounted on the fronts of supermarket shopping carts.

The same is also true for signs on the sides of buses or on top of taxis, posters in city bus shelters or on commuter train platforms, and illuminated signs that line the corridors of airports.

Billboard Production

Most of the big highway signs that are part of national or large regional campaigns are printed on many different sheets of paper and pasted on boards. The sizes of the signs are denoted by the number of sheets they use. Common sizes are 8-sheet, a fairly small board usually seen in cities, and 32-sheet, the smallest of the highway boards.

If you actually have to produce an outdoor board someday and the place where you work has no print production manager, the Outdoor Advertising Institute will give you all of the necessary mechanical information. Don't think about the production mechanics of outdoor. Focus on the concept. It will be the greatest challenge your campaign concept will have to face.

In this chapter you've seen why outdoor advertising is a creative challenge, both to you and to the campaign you have created. Most important, you've learned how to use it as a test of the true value of an idea.

Part Six

The Bottom Line for You

CHAPTER 14

How to Get a Job in Advertising

It's time to remind you that creating advertising isn't just a craft, it's a job. And you should start preparing now to find your first job. To do this, you need a *book*, which is what we call the portfolio of *spec* (speculative) ads you've created.

The Book on the Book

Putting your book together is a tough assignment. Telling you how to do it can take an entire actual book. Lucky for you, the book has been written, insightfully, clearly, and, in my opinion, perfectly, by Maxine Paetro. It's called *How to Put Your Book Together and Get a Job in Advertising*. If you can't find it in a library or your local bookstore, you can buy one from The Copy Workshop at 2144 North Hudson, Chicago, IL 60614.

My Notes for Your Book

Meanwhile, I'll give you a few of my own ideas about what a portfolio should do. The purpose of a portfolio is not to prove that you studied advertising at school. Its purpose is to show that you are a smart, disciplined, energetic, and singular talent who will be an asset to the interviewer's organization.

What to Include

If you're really proud of some of the work you did in your creative courses, that work should go into the portfolio. But be sure it was thoroughly thought through. For example, one of your best pieces may be a single ad. If the concept of the ad is strong enough to support a full ad campaign, then create the campaign, even if that's not what you were asked to do in school.

For portfolio purposes, a campaign should consist of three full-page consumer magazine ads, two or three newspaper or magazine small-space ads, one TV commercial, and one outdoor board. You might want to write a radio commercial, too, but don't be surprised if nobody wants to read it.

Your portfolio needs one complete campaign as its centerpiece, and I do mean *center*. If you open with the campaign, the rest of the portfolio will look spotty. If you close with it, the person viewing your portfolio may never get to it, because you may have already given the impression that all you can do is one-shot ads.

I suggest that you start with five or six individual ads, each for a different product or service. Next, show your campaign. Then show another three or four more of your best full-page one-shots. Finally, finish up with a little burst of fireworks in the form of five or six small-space ads and a couple of outdoor boards, all for products or services not previously shown in the portfolio.

The Right Format

The form that I prefer for a book is actually not a book at all. I like to see each ad mounted on foam board or illustration board and protected by acetate. The small-space ads can be grouped, though no more than four should be placed on one page. Be sure that your name, set in bold type, appears on the back of each ad. By the time the interviewer has turned over all of those ads, there won't be any question about who did them.

The boards should be put in a square-edged, rigid, lightweight art case. These are available in art supply stores. Put the boards in so they appear in the order in which you will want them seen. In any decent interview, the order will be completely disrupted. Be sure you reorganize everything before your book gets shown again.

I prefer this form to the loose-leaf portfolio with black "scrapbook" pages between acetates for several reasons. It's hard for me to read through the flare of acetate pages laid out on my desk. It's much easier to read through acetate if I can hold the page in my hand at an angle that avoids the flare. When I hold your ad in my hand, I somehow become more involved in it and, thus, in you. Finally, in the loose-leaf format, you lose the opportunity to put your name on the back of each board and in the front of my mind.

When you make up your book, you should make three or more copies of it. The reason for this is that, when looking for a copywriter or art director, most ad agencies will ask to keep the book for a few days. This often turns out to be a few weeks. If you have only one book, this will stop your job search cold. You need at least two books in circulation and one in your possession for unplanned, last-minute opportunities.

The First Job

Now, let's consider that first job. You're probably thinking about ad agencies with national accounts, plenty of TV with big production budgets, and big salaries for young creative geniuses. It can work that way, but the odds are against it. Most of us have had to start by doing something else, like being a typist in an agency's creative department or working in the mail room.

My Story

I think my own history is pretty typical. I didn't study advertising in college; I studied literature and history. I couldn't find a job in advertising, not even in the mail room. I reluctantly took a job as an executive trainee in a big department store. I began my writing career as editor of the store's house organ.

Then I got a job in the advertising department of an electronics manufacturer. My primary responsibility was to edit their house organ, but I was also allowed to write a few trade ads. Next I worked in the sales promotion department of a magazine. Then I moved on to another magazine.

Along the way, I met a lot of people in advertising and was able to do a fair number of freelance jobs, which became the base for my portfolio. This got me a job in a tiny, financially unstable ad agency where I did everything: copywriting, print production, art buying, media planning, the works.

When the agency folded, I freelanced full-time. My biggest client was a mail-order dress company for which I wrote catalog copy. Then I found a copywriting job at an agency that specialized in pharmaceutical advertising read by doctors. Next, I worked for CBS as Advertising Director of the radio network.

Finally, I got a job at a real ad agency, Doyle Dane Bernbach, the very best of its day. I was finally where I wanted to be, and it had only taken me seven years of job-hopping.

Don't Be too Picky

If you have no luck with ad agencies, consider some of these jobs as starting places. Look for learning (and earning) opportunities at magazines and newspapers, in TV and radio stations' sales promotion departments, in manufacturers' ad management departments, in retail stores' ad departments, at direct response agencies, at sales promotion agencies, and in public relations firms.

If these look like awful fates after going to college and preparing for the big time, consider the alternatives. Would you rather work at a fast-food restaurant? Or at K-Mart? Or selling encyclopedias door-to-door? Be grateful for any first job you can get that uses your knowledge of advertising and your skills as a communicator. It may well be the key that opens the door to the big time.

Afterword

I'm sure you now know a lot more than you did when you first opened this book. Mostly, I hope that you know more about yourself. You know that you can both draw and write. You know that you can think visually. You know, too, that even if you can't do any of these things very well yet, you can already do them well enough to help you communicate better. And you know that you'll get more skilled as you practice, because thinking visually isn't a gift or a talent but a learned skill.

If I've helped you to learn those things, I'm happy I wrote this book. While writing it, I developed an image of you, and I've enjoyed spending time with you. Now it's time for me to say good-bye. I've got to get back to work. And so do you.

Glossary

Animatic. A detailed and well-drawn videotaped storyboard with a sound track that is used to test commercials.

Apples. Boxes used to raise props, cameras, or anything else.

Art. Anything other than type that will appear in a finished ad.

Ascenders. The upright parts of lowercase letters that stand higher than the body of the letters.

Assistant cameraman. Responsible for mechanical operation of camera, lenses, film magazine, etc.

Assistant director. Assists the director, but doesn't direct.

Barn doors. Flaps on the sides of stage lights.

Beauty shot. A shot that shows the product.

Body copy. The main copy in an ad.

Bold lead. A paragraph that starts the body copy, set in bold type, that makes the main selling point(s) of the ad.

Book. Your portfolio.

Callback. A second look at an actor.

Clapper. Slap-stick on slate used to give audiovisual cues.

Continuity. Keeps track of timing on all takes, marks those to be printed, and is responsible for the logic of the commercial.

Cross-head. Small headlines that are placed strategically through a long-copy ad.

CU. Close-up.

Cut. (verb) "Stop the take." Only the director and the sound person are allowed to give this command.

Cut. (noun) An abrupt end to a scene followed instantly by the abrupt start of another.

Dailies. Overnight film prints.

Demographics. Facts about a target group, such as age, income, race, demographic distribution, ages of children at home, education level, etc.

Descenders. The upright parts of lowercase letters that hang below the body of the letters.

Director. Individual responsible for everything in the shoot.

Direct response. Advertising that asks for an immediate order, such as coupon ads, mail-order catalogs and letters, TV spots asking viewers to call in their order, etc.

Dissolve. A scene fading out as another fades in.

ECU. Extreme close-up.

Flag. A card held on a grip stand to deflect light.

Flatbed. An editing machine.

Gaffers. Lighting technicians.

Gels. Colored inserts in front of a spot.

Grips. All-purpose studio and location craftspeople.

Grip stand. A multipurpose device used to hold things in place.

Heads and tails. Excess frames at the beginning and end of a take that allow flexibility in editing.

In the clear. Anything in a sound track, voice, music, or SFX, that is heard alone, without interference from another sound.

Italic. Slanted type.

Justified. Type with all lines the same length until the end of a paragraph.

Key Grip. The boss of the grips.

Key frame board. A one-frame storyboard that shows a major scene, gives full descriptions of other scenes, and outlines voice, SFX, and music specs.

Legs. Description of a campaign theme that can be executed in every medium.

Lighting director. Individual who plans and executes the lighting.

Limbo. A still or moving picture shot against seamless paper.

Line art. Art or type that will not be screened in engraving.

Line up. Synchronize film with voice, SFX, and music tracks.

Mag. The magazine, which holds the film as it feeds into the camera.

Master. A central scene that is returned to several times.

MCU. Medium close-up.

Mechanical. The elements of a print ad pasted in position or overlaid in position on acetate to be photoengraved.

Mix. Assemble all elements in final order and volume.

Mortise. Appears as an opening cut into a scene, usually as a place to put type.

Mooz. The reverse of a zoom.

Moviola. An editing machine.

Music bed. Music heard through a spot, played at a low level.

Operator. Another (genderless) word for cameraman.

Pan. A lateral camera move that is made by turning the camera on its tripod.

Photomatic. An animatic made with photos.

Plates. The photoengraving(s) from which an ad is printed.

Pool out. The description of a campaign that invites many different executions.

Positioning statement. How you want your target to think of the advertised product or service.

Pre-pro. The preproduction meeting that starts the production process.

Psychographics. Nonstatistical facts about a target group, such as lifestyle, aspirations, mood when using the product or service, etc.

Proof. An engraver's sample printing of the plate(s).

Qualitative research. Research that is not statistically projectable but is directionally useful. This research typically takes the form of consumer focus groups.

Rag right or left. Typeset to meet a straight margin on either the right or left, with the other side left ragged.

Register. The alignment of color plates in a proof.

Re-set. Making a new camera and lighting set-up.

Run-around. Typeset to run around the form of an illustration.

Roman. Type that stands upright. Usually reserved for serif type faces.

San serif. Type faces without serifs.

Separation. The process of converting continuous tone color art into red, yellow, blue, and black screen dot plates. Proofs from these plates are called separations.

Serif. Typefaces with small horizontal marks on the tops and bottoms of the characters.

Set. The place the shooting is done, whether on location or in a studio.

Selects. The scenes from the dailies that you want to be printed as work prints for editing.

Set-up. Each time the camera is moved on the set, or to another set, and the lighting is readjusted.

Scene. A particular piece of action.

Scratch track. A rough recording made as a shooting and editing guide.

SFX. Sound effects.

Shooting storyboard. A director's board of one frame per second used to indicate more precise timing of scenes.

Show reel. A selection of commercials by which a director is judged.

Silks. Inserts in front of a spot to diffuse light.

Slate. A board with taped-on numbers that is filmed before each take. The slate is used to keep track of scene and take numbers.

Slug. A blank piece of film used to indicate the position and time-length or size of a missing optical.

Spec ads. Ads done for your portfolio.

Speed. Sound recording is running.

Strike. Dismantle a set.

Super. Words superimposed on film.

Swipe. The use of existing illustrations or photos for layout purposes.

Tabletop. Describes photographers and directors who specialize in food.

Take. Whenever film (or tape) is in use. There may be many takes of a scene.

Talent. Actors.

Target market. The people to whom you will direct your advertising.

Title. Type on black or white that is cut into the film or tape or used at the beginning or end of a spot.

Thumbnail. A rough layout that is smaller than the actual size of the finished ad.

Verbatims. Direct quotes from focus group participants.

V.O. Voice over, or someone unseen talking.

Widow. The last line of a paragraph that looks too short.

Working storyboard. A board containing as many frames as it takes to show all scenes; that indicates cuts, dissolves, supers, mortises, etc.; provides copy, SFX, and music specs; and gives action descriptions.

Wrap. The completion of a shoot or a shooting day.

Zoom. A camera move that makes the scene appear to come closer. (The reverse of a zoom is called a mooz.)

About the Author

A veteran of thirty-seven years in advertising, David Herzbrun was Founder and Creative Director of Doyle Dane Bernbach's foreign operations in the early 1960s. He returned to Europe in 1981-82 as Executive Creative Director/Europe for J. Walter Thompson. Mr. Herzbrun also served as Creative Director at Ogilvy & Mather (USA) and at Humphrey Browning McDougall (Boston). He returned to Doyle Dane Bernbach in the position of Senior Vice President and World-Wide Creative Supervisor of the agency's International Division. At the time of his retirement, he was serving as Executive Vice President, Group Creative Director, and a member of the Board of Directors for Saatchi & Saatchi Compton.

Mr. Herzbrun has won nearly two hundred major awards for his work, both in the U.S. and abroad, including The Cannes Film Festival, Clio, Andy, One Show, and New England Hatch Awards. His classic Volkswagen "Snowplow" spot, a First at Cannes, is the first commercial ever to be included in the Permanent Film Collection of the Museum of Modern Art in New York.

His memoir, *Playing in Traffic on Madison Avenue*, was published in 1990.